Columbia University

Contributions to Education

Teachers College Series

No. 842

AMS PRESS
NEW YORK

UNIT COSTS

OF SCHOOL BUILDINGS

By

Henry Hubener Bormann

SUBMITTED IN PARTIAL FULFILLMENT OF THE REQUIREMENTS
FOR THE DEGREE OF DOCTOR OF PHILOSOPHY IN THE
FACULTY OF PHILOSOPHY, COLUMBIA UNIVERSITY

Published with the Approval of
Professor N. L. Engelhardt, Sponsor

221899

BUREAU OF PUBLICATIONS

Teachers College · Columbia University

NEW YORK · 1941

Library of Congress Cataloging in Publication Data

Bormann, Henry Hubener, 1905-
   Unit costs of school buildings.

   Reprint of the 1941 ed., issued in series: Teachers
College, Columbia University. Contributions to edu-
cation, no. 842.
   Originally presented as the author's thesis, Columbia.
   Bibliography: p.
   1. School buildings--United States. 2. Education--
United States--Finance. 3. Building--Estimates.
I. Title. II. Series: Columbia University. Teachers
College. Contributions to education, no. 842.
LB3209.B6 1972   338.5'1   78-176582
ISBN 0-404-55842-9

Reprinted by Special Arrangement with Teachers
College Press, New York, New York

From the edition of 1941, New York
First AMS edition published in 1972
Manufactured in the United States

AMS PRESS, INC.
NEW YORK, N. Y.   10003

Acknowledgments

To Professor N. L. Engelhardt, his sponsor, the author is deeply indebted for the inspiration, encouragement, and guidance which made this study possible. The invaluable assistance of Professors Helen M. Walker, Ralph B. Spence, Willard S. Elsbree, Kenneth A. Smith, and William H. Hayes is also gratefully acknowledged.

Without the cooperation of Dr. W. K. Wilson, Dr. Don L. Essex, and other members of the State Education Department this study could not have been made. Their cooperation is appreciated.

For constant encouragement and many helpful suggestions, the author is especially grateful to Dr. Howard T. Herber, Superintendent of Schools, Malverne, New York, and to Dr. N. L. Engelhardt, Jr., Assistant Director of Research, Newark Public Schools, Newark, New Jersey.

H. H. B.

Contents

UNIT COSTS
OF SCHOOL BUILDINGS

Chapter I

Introduction and Purpose of the Study

Introduction. An intensive and extensive national study of school finance was authorized by Congress in 1931 when a sum of $50,000 was made available in the appropriation of the Department of the Interior for the first year of a four-year National Survey of School Finance. Those in charge of the survey made detailed plans for the entire program. Work had scarcely begun, however, when it became apparent that an economy-minded Congress would make no appropriation for the following year. It was necessary to terminate the survey in the best way possible under the circumstances. The result was the publication of *Research Problems in School Finance*, from which the following is quoted:

> Faced with the necessity of discontinuing work on the survey at an early date, it was decided in conference with the Board of Consultants to develop that feature of the original plans which outlined the promotion of cooperative research. Accordingly, it was decided to prepare a brief monograph which might be placed in the hands of research students interested in school finance, which would furnish them suggestions concerning topics from which they might choose to carry on research, which would afford them an insight into the objectives that might properly be set up for their studies, and would give them a better conception of possible research in school finance and of the social basis upon which the entire subject rests. [1:4]*

Chapter IV of this monograph stressed the need for research directed toward the improvement of existing units of expen-

---

* Throughout the text, numbers in brackets refer to the Bibliography on pages 82 to 83. The number preceding the colon indicates the reference; the number following the colon indicates the page cited in the reference.

diture measurement in school finance and the development of
unit expenditure measures related to specific categories of service. The use of such units in studies of comparative costs is a
chief means of analyzing expenditures and detecting waste.

Of course, possibilities for waste of money exist in every expenditure, public or private. Education is no exception. The
vastness and complexity of the enterprise of public education
in the United States multiply the chances for injudicious spend-
ing of money. Even though the expenditure of money for
public education is directed by a group of men and women
who are, on the whole, conscientious, honest, and comparatively
efficient, continuous study of school finance is necessary. Such
study is the best assurance of constant progress, steady increase
in efficiency and economy, and continuous improvement of the
financial structure for the organization and administration of
public education.

Expenditures for capital outlay. Capital outlay is the second
largest item of school cost. It is exceeded only by expenditure
for teachers' salaries. Capital outlay includes all expenditures
which add to the permanent school property not consumed in
use, such as land, buildings, furniture, and equipment. In recent years it has been estimated that approximately $400,-
000,000 is spent annually for capital outlay in the schools of
the United States. [1 : 96] It has further been estimated that
more than three-fourths of this expenditure is for new school
buildings. [1 : 97]

In the even-numbered years from 1930 to 1936 inclusive, a
total of $812,472,463 was spent for school buildings, grounds,
and equipment in the United States. An additional expenditure of $502,790,340 was made to meet interest charges neces-
sitated by capital outlay. [2 : 33] Assuming the same average
annual expenditure of funds for capital outlay and interest
charges in the odd-numbered years between 1931 and 1937
inclusive, the estimated total expenditure for capital outlay
and interest charges for school buildings, grounds, and equipment in the United States for the years 1930 to 1937 inclusive
was $2,630,525,606.

In New York State alone, during the years 1930 to 1937 inclusive, a total of $305,588,980 was spent for school buildings, grounds, and equipment. [3:48] This amount did not include interest charges.

Research in school building costs. In spite of the large expenditures of money for school building construction, the number of research studies of school building costs has been surprisingly small. The *Review of Educational Research* in October, 1938, reported only thirteen research studies on the cost of school buildings, exclusive of finance, maintenance, and operation. [4:408-12, 480-81] At that time Herber's *The Influence of the Public Works Administration on School Building Construction in New York State* [5] had not been published, and Engelhardt, Jr.'s study of school building costs [6] had not been started.

Need for a study of unit cost measures. In view of the limited amount of research which had been carried on and the areas in which that research had been conducted, a study of unit cost measures for school building construction seemed to be needed. Such a study appeared to be in line with the recommendations of the National Survey of School Finance, because the study would aim to improve existing units of expenditure measurement and to develop possible new expenditure measures for school building construction costs. Knowledge derived from such a study seemed to be basic to an understanding of the values and limitations of the units in terms of which other cost studies might be made.

Preliminary investigation disclosed that architects and educators had long been dissatisfied with some of the units used for expressing and comparing school building costs. These men felt that certain units commonly used failed to provide a fair basis for comparing building costs.

Need for comparative cost data. Lack of well-defined, clearly understood, and generally accepted units of expenditure measurement has made comparative study of school building costs difficult. Inadequate knowledge of comparative costs has been a fundamental weakness in the educational administration of school building construction. In 1915 Ittner regretted the lack of "reliable data on the cost of school buildings, from which general information can be deduced for comparison between the costs of buildings for various communities." [7:69] Evidence that the need has persisted is found in the following quotation from Moehlman nineteen years later:

> One of the most important problems in the field of the school plant is to determine a means whereby adequate and valid cost data may be secured and used not only for immediate needs but also over a long-time period for comparative studies. [8:309]

Difficulty in securing comparative data. Collins [9:19] declared in 1914 that it seemed as if quotations of actual costs of various schools were presented more for magazine reading than for real use. He found many reported costs interesting because they were complete and evidently accurate, but many also were useless from the standpoint of application to other work.

Baldwin attributed the difficulty to lack of a uniform and accepted unit of measurement.

> It is now almost impossible to compare the work of one architect or engineer with that of another, or to measure in precise terms the results of their efforts. When an attempt is made to compare the cost of one building with the cost of another, we often find ourselves utterly helpless because of a lack of a unit of measurement which is uniform, standard, and generally accepted. [10:22]

Value of cost data. In 1915 Ittner [7:69] pointed out that, if data on the cost of school buildings in various communities could be collected and reduced to a reasonably comparable basis, such data would prove of great value in determining the amounts of money needed for new buildings and the amounts of proposed bond issues needed to carry out definite building programs.

A few years later Donovan wrote:

> There are two distinct purposes in seeking to determine the costs of school buildings: one to enable boards of education to provide with some degree of accuracy sufficient funds for the erection and

equipment of new buildings, and the other to determine, by comparison with the costs of similar structures before the board has obligated itself by contracts, the economy to be exercised in the planning and construction of the proposed work. The former is essential to good business management, and the latter is a necessary precaution against extravagance. [11 : 70]

The literature of unit costs of school buildings. A review of the literature of unit costs of school buildings revealed that various measures of the size or capacity of a school building are in current use. Building size or capacity is sometimes measured in terms of a unit of volume, such as the cubic foot, or in terms of a unit of area, such as the square foot of floor area, or in terms of a unit of educational space, such as the pupil station. At least nine such units of measure have been proposed. The measures of building size or capacity resulting from the application of the different units of measure are:

1. Total cubature
2. Habitable cubature
3. Educational cubature
4. Total floor area
5. Habitable floor area
6. Educational floor area
7. Number of classrooms
8. Pupil capacity
9. Number of pupil stations

When the total cost of a school building is divided by the number of units in a particular measure applied to the building, the resulting quotient is a unit cost. This unit cost indicates the cost of school building construction per unit of size or capacity. The units of cost corresponding to the measures listed above are:

1. Cost per cubic foot
2. Cost per cubic foot of habitable cubature
3. Cost per cubic foot of educational cubature
4. Cost per square foot of floor area
5. Cost per square foot of habitable floor area
6. Cost per square foot of educational floor area

7. Cost per classroom
8. Cost per pupil
9. Cost per pupil station

The measures of building size or capacity may be used as bases for estimating the cost of proposed school buildings. The units of cost may be used for comparing the costs of school buildings.

A summary was made of statements of the advantages and disadvantages of the various units. This summary was based on criticisms appearing in books, magazine articles, and published speeches. The statements represented the opinions of school architects, school administrators, college professors, and others whose experience in school building planning and construction made their opinions worthy of consideration. These statements were not always in agreement.

The purpose of the study. The purpose of this study has been to evaluate in an impartial, objective manner the nine measures of building size or capacity and the nine units of cost mentioned above. There has been no published evidence of any attempt to do this previously. This study has attempted to answer the following questions:

1. What are the advantages and disadvantages of the various units applied to school building costs?
2. Which measure of building size or capacity is best suited for use in estimating the cost of a proposed building?
3. Which unit of cost is best suited for comparing school building costs?
4. Can a new unit be developed which will be more satisfactory than those now used?

This study brings together the opinions of men whose work as architects or educators has led them to think about the problems incident to making fair and revealing comparisons among school building construction costs. In discussing the suitability of units of cost, writers in this field have criticized various units and have proposed others. They have tried to indicate the disadvantages of the cost units of which they disapprove and have claimed corresponding advantages for one or more units whose use they favor. Some of these statements can be accepted without question; they are obviously true. Others, however, cannot be accepted without question.

As part of this study, statements regarding the units of cost were tested to see if they were in agreement with the data presented. Some of these statements were found untenable in the light of relationships discovered in this study. Other statements were confirmed by the findings of this study.

This raises the question of the applicability of the results of this study. Do the results apply to other groups of school buildings built under other physical conditions and designed to satisfy other legal and educational requirements?

The group of New York State buildings studied was not a random sample of all school buildings in the United States. Many schools in other states are built under physical conditions very different from those in New York State. Differing educational needs and programs in other states also affect school building construction. On the other hand, in considering the applicability of the results of this study, it should be recognized that the New York State buildings studied are reasonably representative of current school building construction. These buildings are safe, sanitary, attractive, and well constructed. It is reasonable to assume that measures of building size or capacity and units of cost suited to these buildings will also prove helpful in studying the costs of groups of school buildings in other states. This will be especially true if studies of school building construction costs elsewhere are confined to separate states. In statewide studies, school building costs will not be influenced by varying laws and regulations affecting school organization and building construction. Even climate, which influences building design and construction to a considerable extent, is less variable within the borders of a given state. The applicability of this study is further discussed in a later chapter.

If a larger number of buildings had been studied, it might have been possible to develop norms of expenditure. This was, however, not the purpose of this study and not feasible under the conditions of the study. This study required that complete plans, specifications, and cost data be available for each building; that an enormous amount of detail work be done to get data from the plans and specifications; and that the buildings studied be restricted to one state in order that some of the variables associated with costs of school buildings could be held constant. Therefore, no norms of expenditure were developed. This is also further discussed in a later chapter.

Chapter II

Sources of Data and General Procedure

Introduction. At the time this study was planned, Engelhardt, Jr. was contemplating a study of school buildings in New York State in an effort to discover the elements of design and construction which were related to variations in the cost of these buildings. [6:5] The writer was interested in studying unit costs of school buildings to determine: (1) the advantages and disadvantages of applying various units to school building costs; (2) which measure of building size or capacity is best suited for use in estimating the cost of a proposed building; (3) which unit of cost is best suited for comparing school building costs; and (4) whether a new unit could be developed which would be more satisfactory than those now used.

It was anticipated that the findings of Engelhardt, Jr. regarding the extent to which various construction factors influence cost could be utilized to correct the total costs of the buildings so that the effects of these construction factors would be eliminated. This would facilitate the study of relationships between the unit costs and other factors. It was decided, therefore, that the same group of buildings would be used for each study.

The writer worked with Engelhardt, Jr. in gathering the basic data [6:v] with the understanding that some of these data would also be used for the writer's study which was to follow. The enormous amount of detail work involved in taking data from the plans and specifications for each building was further justification for this procedure.

Buildings studied. Eight elementary schools, six secondary schools, and thirty-eight combined elementary and secondary

9

schools constituted the group of fifty-two school buildings studied. These were the school buildings constructed in New York State between 1930 and 1937 for which complete plans, specifications, and cost data were obtained from the School Buildings and Grounds Division of the New York State Education Department. One-room and two-room buildings of wood-frame construction and additions to existing buildings were excluded.

Table

Costs and Major Characteristics of

Building Number	Total Cost in Hundreds of Dollars *	Total Cubature in Thousands of Cubic Feet	Date of Construction	Type of School **	Number of Floors Above Basement	Constructed Under P.W.A.
1	452	175	1935	E	1	No
2	552	124	1935	E	1	Yes
3	604	152	1933	E	1	No
4	712	213	1930	C	2	No
5	789	248	1934	E	2	Yes
6	894	296	1934	C	2	Yes
7	992	332	1934	E	1	Yes
8	1,056	358	1930	C	2	No
9	1,059	369	1931	C	2	No
10	1,140	378	1931	C	2	No
11	1,160	299	1935	E	2	Yes
12	1,172	403	1935	C	2	Yes
13	1,295	401	1934	C	2	Yes
14	1,325	401	1931	C	2	No
15	1,349	394	1935	C	2	Yes
16	1,416	537	1934	C	2	Yes
17	1,530	520	1935	S	2	Yes
18	1,533	525	1931	C	2	No
19	1,691	438	1931	E	2	No
20	1,727	602	1930	C	2	No
21	1,737	601	1936	C	2	No
22	1,773	583	1932	C	2	No
23	1,789	541	1931	C	2	No
24	1,813	582	1936	C	2	Yes
25	1,846	691	1935	C	2	No
26	1,883	523	1935	C	2	Yes

* Cost includes only general construction, heating and ventilating, plumbing,
** Type of school: E = elementary school; S = secondary school; C = combined

Characteristics of the buildings. The buildings ranged in size from 124,000 cubic feet to 1,950,000 cubic feet and in cost from $45,200 to $529,900. Table 1 shows the cost and major characteristics of each building included in the study. Plans and specifications for these buildings had been approved by the New York State Education Department. The smallest building was a modern, flat-roofed, brick elementary school with three classrooms, assembly-lunch room, boys' toilet, girls' toilet,

THE BUILDINGS INCLUDED IN THIS STUDY

Building Number	Total Cost in Hundreds of Dollars *	Total Cubature in Thousands of Cubic Feet	Date of Construction	Type of School **	Number of Floors Above Basement	Constructed Under P.W.A.
27	1,966	590	1937	C	2	Yes
28	1,991	569	1930	C	2	No
29	2,014	500	1932	E	2	No
30	2,212	704	1935	C	2	Yes
31	2,222	763	1932	C	2	No
32	2,291	782	1935	C	2	Yes
33	2,322	721	1931	C	2	No
34	2,376	842	1934	C	2	Yes
35	2,400	948	1934	S	3	Yes
36	2,419	770	1934	S	2	Yes
37	2,429	795	1931	C	3	No
38	2,439	950	1932	C	2	No
39	2,589	804	1930	C	2	No
40	2,615	733	1935	C	2	Yes
41	2,729	848	1930	C	3	No
42	2,782	900	1930	C	2	No
43	2,817	890	1934	S	3	Yes
44	2,876	905	1936	C	3	Yes
45	3,002	1,170	1935	C	3	No
46	3,042	1,270	1932	S	3	No
47	3,203	923	1935	S	2	Yes
48	3,290	1,005	1930	C	2	No
49	3,668	1,216	1936	C	2	Yes
50	4,205	1,153	1933	C	3	Yes
51	4,628	1,300	1937	C	2	Yes
52	5,299	1,950	1936	C	2	Yes

and electrical work.
elementary and secondary school.

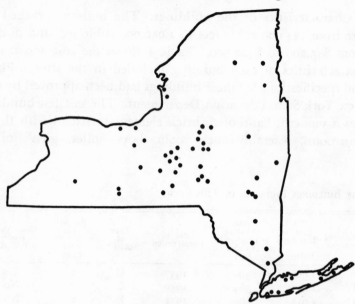

MAP 1. Locations of the Fifty-Two School Buildings Included
in This Study

teachers' room, boiler room, and fuel storage room. The largest
building was an attractive colonial structure housing a combined elementary and secondary school with twenty-two classrooms, kindergarten, shop, commercial room, art room, science
room, laboratory, study hall, library, model apartment, auditorium, gymnasium, locker and shower rooms, cafeteria,
kitchen, and many special offices, rooms, and facilities.

Exactly half of the buildings were constructed with the financial assistance and accompanying supervision of the Public
Works Administration. The costs of half of the buildings were,
therefore, subjected to the influence of that Administration. [5]
The buildings were erected in communities of less than fifty
thousand population scattered throughout New York State.
Map 1 shows the locations of the fifty-two school buildings.

Plan analysis. Engelhardt, Jr. and the writer, working together, obtained the following basic data for each building:

1. Total cubature
2. Total floor area

3. Linear feet of perimeter of the building
4. Square feet of ground area covered by the building
5. Cubature of all rooms and spaces
6. Floor area of all rooms and spaces
7. Number of floors above basement
8. Square feet of radiation
9. Number and type of plumbing outlets and fixtures
10. Number and type of electrical outlets and fixtures
11. Type of roof
12. Basic materials of construction
13. Interior finish materials.

In addition to these data, the writer determined for each building:
1. Number of classrooms
2. Pupil capacity of building
3. Number of pupil stations of various types

From these basic data the writer then determined for each building:
1. Total habitable cubature
2. Total educational cubature
3. Total educational floor area
4. Per cent of habitable cubature
5. Per cent of educational cubature
6. Per cent of educational floor area
7. Ratio of perimeter to ground area
8. Ratio of perimeter to total cubature
9. Ratio of ground area to total cubature
10. Mean cubature per auditorium pupil station
11. Mean cubature per gymnasium pupil station
12. Mean cubature per auditorium-gymnasium pupil station
13. Mean cubature per bleacher pupil station
14. Mean cubature per cafeteria pupil station
15. Number of weighted pupil stations (weighted in terms of area and cubature)
16. Number of further-weighted pupil stations (weighted in terms of area, cubature, and cost per cubic foot)

Building costs. The basic cost data were obtained by Engelhardt, Jr. and the writer from the files of the School Buildings and Grounds Division of the New York State Education Department. The exact recording and clear segregation of costs in the Department records made it possible to use total costs which included the same items of cost for each building.

For the purposes of this study the total cost of construction included:

1. Cost of the general construction contract
2. Cost of the heating and ventilating contract
3. Cost of the plumbing contract
4. Cost of the electrical contract
5. Other contract and non-contract costs which contributed to the expense of general construction, heating and ventilating, plumbing, or electrical work

General procedure. In order to determine which measure of building size or capacity is best suited for use in estimating the cost of a proposed building, the school buildings used in this study were measured in terms of each, and these measures were then correlated with the total costs of the buildings. As a further check on the correlations, the costs of twenty-five buildings were estimated on the basis of each measure of building size or capacity.

The procedure for determining which unit of cost is best suited for use in comparing costs of school buildings was suggested by the following quotation from Shigley:

That one architect can materially reduce the unit cost of construction over that of another without altering quality is, of course, preposterous. The superior architect excels in the adaptation of his construction to the purposes for which the building is to be used and the consequent economy of both space and material. In thus securing efficient planning, the client finds maximum service at minimum cost that dwarfs into insignificance minor savings made here and there in the possible substitution of less expensive and frequently untried building materials. [12 : 43]

Unit costs of school buildings are determined, in the first instance, by quality of construction. Other things being equal, lowering the quality of construction lowers the unit cost, and raising the quality of construction raises the unit cost. But costs are also influenced by skillful planning. The superior architect creates a more efficient design from both a structural and an educational point of view.

The various units of cost are not equally effective in revealing these differences in efficiency of designing and planning and in educational serviceability. Yet, this is exactly the effectiveness which is needed in a unit of cost used for comparative purposes. The best unit to use in comparing school building construction costs is the one which is most closely related to measures of efficiency of designing and planning and to measures of educational serviceability.

In this study the units of cost were studied in relation to efficiency of designing and planning of the buildings. The units of cost were correlated with four measures of efficiency of designing and planning. The units of cost were also studied in relation to the educational serviceability of the buildings by correlating them with two measures of educational service ability. The measures of building size or capacity were also correlated with a measure of educational serviceability. These criteria will be elaborated later.

Correcting the costs. In order to study the measures of building size or capacity and units of cost as described above, it was desirable to eliminate as many as possible of the variations in costs due to other factors.

To eliminate the effect of variations in wages and materials prices, the costs of general construction, heating and ventilating, plumbing, and electrical work were corrected by means of indices developed for this group of buildings by Engelhardt, Jr. [6] Each of the four basic construction costs was corrected separately by means of the appropriate index. The four corrected costs for each building were then added to form total costs of construction corrected for variations in wages and materials prices.

These total costs were then further corrected for variations due to type of construction, roof construction, and grade of

interior finish. Finally, the total costs were corrected for variations due to general plan type. These corrections were based
on the findings of Engelhardt, Jr. and were made in the manner
which he describes. [6 : 43, 46]

These successive corrections of total costs made possible the
study of the measures of building size or capacity and units
of cost at three separate stages as the effects of variations due
to construction factors were eliminated.

Unit costs. On the basis of total costs corrected for variations in wages and materials prices, type of construction, roof
construction, and grade of interior finish, the writer calculated
the following unit costs for each building:

1. Cost per cubic foot
2. Cost per cubic foot of habitable cubature
3. Cost per cubic foot of educational cubature
4. Cost per square foot of floor area
5. Cost per square foot of habitable floor area
6. Cost per square foot of educational floor area
7. Cost per classroom
8. Cost per pupil
9. Cost per pupil station
10. Cost per weighted pupil station
11. Cost per further-weighted pupil station

Unit costs were similarly calculated for each building on the
basis of costs corrected for variations in wages and materials
prices, type of construction, roof construction, grade of interior
finish, and general plan type.

Chapter III

Cost per Cubic Foot

Introduction. The most generally accepted and widely used unit for comparing construction costs of school buildings is the cost per cubic foot. It is simple in concept and easy to calculate. First, the total volume within the outside surfaces of a building is measured in cubic feet. Then the total cost of construction is divided by the total number of cubic feet. This gives the cost per cubic foot.

Methods of calculating the cubature of a building differ in detail. In any comparative study the particular method adopted must be precisely defined and uniformly applied. In this study total cubature was calculated on the basis of the formula established by the School Buildings and Grounds Division of the New York State Education Department. This method of estimating cubature was applied to each building. The estimates were checked with figures filed with the State Department.

The State Department rules for cubature are as follows:

1. Prepare a separate diagram to scale for each of the following sections of the building: (*a*) basement areas; (*b*) principal stories; (*c*) roof areas; and (*d*) other areas, such as cupolas, penthouses, boiler stacks, porticos, subbasements. Supplement diagrams of areas by such cross sections through the building as are essential to a ready comprehension of the table of calculation of cubature.

2. Calculate separately the areas listed in paragraph 1 (*a*), (*b*), (*c*), and (*d*). First, divide each area into convenient rectangles or other figures. Second, identify each subdivision by letter or other character.

3. Calculate the cubature contained within each cube formed, by taking the area described by outline under paragraph 2, times the height of the section in which such cube occurs.

4. All horizontal areas shall be measured from the outside face of the inclosing walls at the plane of the floor.

5. (*a*) The height of principal stories shall be measured from a horizontal plane two feet below the surface of the finished floor of the first story to the underside of the ceiling of the top story in that section of the building in which the cube occurs which is being calculated.

(*b*) In sections without finished ceilings, the perpendicular dimensions shall be taken from a horizontal plane two feet below the finished floor of the first story to the mean height of roof surface of the section.

6. The height of developed basement areas shall be measured from the surface of the finished basement floor to a horizontal plane two feet below the surface of the finished floor of the first story.

7. Roof areas: (*a*) Parapet roofs (flat roof type) shall be measured from the under side of the ceiling of the top story to a horizontal plane four feet above the underside of the ceiling of the top story.

(*b*) Sloping ridge roofs shall be measured from the underside of the ceiling of the top story to a horizontal plane at the mean height of the sloping roof.

(*c*) Sloping roofs with deck shall be calculated to obtain actual volume of the roof section above the plane of the ceiling of the top story.

8. Other areas: (*a*) The actual volume of towers, cupolas, penthouses, boiler stacks, hoist shafts, area entrances and developed sub-basements shall be obtained. All measurements shall be taken from the outside face to outside face of inclosing walls and from the surface of the floor through to the mean height of roof or inclosing surface.

Note. No cube shall be included more than once. If, for example, a boiler stack is within the principal walls of the building, only that volume which has not been included in 5, 6, and 7, shall be added under this classification.

(*b*) The actual volume of porticos, covered porches, and connecting passageways shall be obtained. Horizontal measurements shall be taken from lines marking the outside of the faces of the frieze of the cornice, or wall structure above columns. Perpendicular measurements shall be taken from mean finished grade to mean height of roof.

9. Uncovered steps, stoops, approaches, buttresses, parapets, light courts, window areas, foundation walls, pipe trenches, cisterns, septic tanks, and retaining walls shall not be calculated nor included.

10. Definitions: (*a*) The principal, or first story, is the lowest story the floor of which is wholly above finished grade at the building.

(*b*) The basement is that portion of the building immediately below the principal, or first story.

(*c*) Neither a basement, a subbasement, nor a cellar shall be termed a "story."

(*d*) A subbasement is that portion of a building which has been developed below the basement level.

(*e*) The mean height is the midpoint between the eaves and the peak of the roof.

Limitations of the cost per cubic foot unit. Cost per cubic foot is subject to several important limitations when used for comparing school building construction costs. It does not indicate whether the volume provided in a building is adequate, of desirable proportion, or arranged for economical and complete utilization. Even if two buildings have the same cubature, differences in shape may affect cost. One building may require more outside wall, or more inside partition, or more roof.

It has been pointed out that cost per cubic foot gives no indication of efficiency of planning. [8:313] A poorly planned building with a considerable amount of excess and useless, but relatively inexpensive cubature, such as wide corridors and stairs, unfinished storerooms, and an empty attic, may appear more economical because of lower cost per cubic foot than a well-planned, compact building in which every space has maximum utility.

Many causes of variation. Collins [9:19] estimated in 1914 that the cost of school buildings ranged from twelve cents to about thirty cents per cubic foot. This he attributed to differences in type of construction, height of ceilings, amount of waste in unproductive space, kind of equipment, definition of cost, and other factors.

Steen [13:112] added the following causes of variation in cost per cubic foot: size and type of structure, location, contractor's desire for profit, forecasting the future market prices of materials and labor, contractor's ability and equipment to handle the job, and the type and ability of subcontractors.

Some practical difficulties. Candidly admitting that even in his own office it is easy to be misled in using cost per cubic foot as a basis for comparing school building costs, Wooldridge gives several illustrations.

A high sloping roof will add tremendously to the cubic contents of a building as compared with a flat roof. The cost per cubic foot may be materially lower, and yet the total cost of the structure will be higher.

Compare a maple floor with sleepers with a linoleum floor laid directly on the structural floor slab. If you maintain a twelve foot clear ceiling height throughout your building and the structure is four stories high, then the maple floor construction superimposed on the structural slab will add approximately one foot to the height of the school. If we apply this example to a building, say 60 feet wide and 300 feet long, we find that this wood floored building contains 18,000 cubic feet more than the linoleum floored building. The cost per cubic foot will be lower and yet the linoleum floored structure with its higher cost per cubic foot will result in a lower total cost.

Take a flat roof building with parapet walls above the roof slab. Let us assume that these parapet walls are five feet high and that the roof slab is laid as close to the top floor ceiling as is practical. (Incidentally, this is a favorite method of reducing the cubage in a school house because the space between the parapets above the roof space is not included as measured cubage, and also, incidentally, it is not good practical design as most maintenance trouble with parapet walls is caused by having both sides exposed to the weather.) Now, let us apply this roof design which I have described to a building 60 feet wide and 300 feet long. If we raise this roof slab to within 18 inches of the top of the parapet walls, we add 63,000 cubic feet to the total structure at relatively small cost, the exterior of the building is not changed a particle, the design, from a maintenance standpoint, is very much better, and yet the cost per cubic foot is materially reduced although the total cost is practically unchanged. So you see, with a cubic foot unit of measurement, we still have to look out for variables even in our own office. [14 : 109-110]

Plan efficiency. Moehlman [8 : 313] declared that cost per cubic foot gives no indication of plan efficiency. As early as 1920, however, Greeley [15 : 159] said that the more expansive and loose the design, the lower will be the cost per cubic foot and the higher the cost per pupil. The more compact the plan, said Greeley, the higher will be the cost per cubic foot and the lower the cost per pupil. Five years earlier Kilham [16 : 107] had said that low cost per cubic foot might be associated, under certain conditions, with high cost per pupil.

Donovan [11 : 79] also warned of the need for checking to be sure that low cost per cubic foot is not accompanied by high cubature per pupil. He said that the compact or closed type of school will have a smaller cubature per pupil, while the open or spread-out type will require a greater allowance; one-story schools will show a decided increase in cubature per pupil over that of two-story or three-story schools. In 1935 Wiley [17 : 17] deplored the fact that cost per cubic foot, the most generally used cost unit, is related in this way to poor planning.

Halsey says:

It is always possible to add empty cubage to a building to reduce the cost per cubic foot, and putting on a pitched roof with an empty or an almost empty attic under it, is one of the easiest ways to do it. [18 : 21] Widening the corridors also helps to do this. [18 : 21]

He gives this illustration:

It is perfectly obvious that the cost per cubic foot of compactly designed first and second stories, when computed together, will be much greater than the cost per cubic foot of an empty attic extending over the entire second story and computed separately. If we then take the cubage of the first and second stories and add the cubage of the empty attic to them, and then compute the cost per cubic foot of these parts of the building together, we will find that it is higher than the cost per cubic foot of the empty attic and lower than the cost per cubic foot of the first and second stories. [18 : 20-21]

Recent research. In a recent study Engelhardt, Jr. related variations in design and construction of school buildings to variations in cost per cubic foot. This study, an investigation of costs, also throws light on the nature of the cost per cubic foot unit. Some of his conclusions are indicated in the following:

Variations in the plan types of the buildings, as measured by relationships of perimeter, ground area, and cubic contents, were significantly related to variations in general construction costs per cubic foot. The cost per cubic foot of a small one-story struc-ture, with open type plan, was estimated to exceed the cost per cubic foot of a large two-story square building by 10 cents per

cubic foot. Buildings with auditoriums above gymnasiums cost
1.2 cents more per cubic foot than buildings with these units located
on the ground-floor level. It was also shown that the changes in
ratio of perimeter to cubic contents were more influential than
changes in the ratio of ground area to cubic contents in determining
the variations in general construction costs per cubic foot. [6 : 86-87]

It was found that the average flat roof, steel-frame building with
face brick and tile exterior walls and tile interior partitions cost
2.3 cents per cubic foot less than flat roof, wall-bearing structures
with face and common brick exterior walls and brick or tile interior
walls. [6 : 87]

Buildings with flat concrete or gypsum slab roofs on steel frame
averaged 2.5 cents per cubic foot more in general construction costs
than buildings with gable or hip roofs on wood frames with slate
covering. [6 : 87]

Average differences in general construction costs per cubic foot
as large as 4.2 cents were found between buildings with different
types of interior finishes. [6 : 87]

Variations in heating and ventilating costs per cubic foot were
influenced principally by variations in the ratios of perimeter to
cubic contents and secondarily by variations in the ratios of ground
area to cubic contents. [6 : 88]

Plumbing and electrical service costs per cubic foot had standard
deviations of 0.5 cents, indicating that these items had small influence on variations in the total costs per cubic foot of the buildings included in the study. The total costs of these services were
largely influenced by the costs of fixtures. [6 : 88-89]

It is apparent that cost per cubic foot is a good unit of measure of the cost of the physical structure of school buildings.
It is sensitive to variations in type of construction, materials
used, and general plan.

Educational serviceability of a school building. An article
appearing in the *American School Board Journal* [19 : 60] ac-
cepts cost per cubic foot as the most dependable index of cost
of the physical structure of a school building, but finds its
main shortcoming in that it does not serve as an index of the
"educational value" of the building. Moehlman states:

The weakness of the cubic foot as a measure of cost from the instructional viewpoint must be apparent. It is a gross measure. It
does not indicate any relation of structure to use, nor does it show
inadequacy or extravagance in design. [8 : 311]

Chapter IV

Units of Cost Other than Cost per Cubic Foot

Introduction. Although school building costs have been compared most frequently on the basis of cost per cubic foot, several other cost units have been used or proposed. Some of these units report costs in terms of measures of the educational serviceability of school buildings. Cost per classroom, cost per pupil, cost per pupil station, cost per cubic foot of educational cubature, and cost per square foot of educational floor area are examples of this type of cost unit. Two of the units report costs in terms of the amount of usable or habitable space. These are cost per cubic foot of habitable cubature and cost per square foot of habitable floor area. One other cost unit is expressed in terms of the total number of square feet of floor area.

Cost per cubic foot of habitable cubature. As early as 1915 Baldwin [10:23-24] suggested a definition of cubature which included only usable space. He defined it as the cubic contents of the spaces or rooms actually used, or available, for school purposes, such as classrooms, coat rooms, assembly halls, corridors, stairways, play rooms, offices, lunch rooms, toilets, storeroom, engine and boiler rooms, coal rooms, stock rooms, fan rooms, but *not* attic spaces or other parts of a building which cannot be used for school or related work.

In order to determine the cost per cubic foot of habitable cubature for a building it is necessary first to find the cubature of each room and space which can be occupied and used for school purposes. This information can be obtained from the complete plans of the building. These cubatures of rooms and spaces are then added to obtain the total habitable cubature.

Finally, the total cost of the building is divided by the total habitable cubature. The resulting quotient is the cost per cubic foot of habitable cubature.

For this study the interior dimensions of all habitable rooms and spaces in each building were read from the plans. The cubatures of all of these rooms and spaces were then calculated, listed, and totaled for each building. The cost per cubic foot of habitable cubature was then figured on this basis.

Cost per cubic foot of educational cubature. Steen further restricts the definition of cubature:

> These rooms, for educational instructional use, are the primary things for which the building is to be built and are definite and known. All other space or volume of a building, such as occurs in corridors, stairs, offices, boiler rooms, coal storage, etc., are merely necessary adjuncts and, as far as size and volume, are variable as the scheme of the plan varies. They are in great measure, therefore, dependent upon the architects' ability to arrange the units of plan compactly and economically. The building which provides the required units for purely educational purposes with satisfactory and sufficient adjuncts at the least cost should be the best plan. The one known and definite factor of cubage with which we have to deal is the cubic foot content of the educational units. [13 : 113]

A similar procedure is reported by Wooldridge. Some of the fixed requirements by which his procedure is guarded are also indicated in the following quotation:

> We compute the total inside air cubage of every academic room. For instance, a class room 22 feet wide by 32 feet long by 12 feet high, contains 8,448 cubic feet. We have definite rules for computing the gymnasiums and all other special academic rooms. The total resulting cubage we call the "Occupational Cubage" and we use this figure as our divisor into the total cost of the building. We do not measure the corridors, stair halls, toilet rooms, administrative rooms, boiler rooms, storage rooms, etc. Of course, the application of this measure is guarded by many fixed requirements which the architect has to meet in designing the building. For instance, he receives very definite instructions as to the administrative rooms required. The number of toilet fixtures on each floor is controlled by State Law, which is also true of the location and number of stairways. We limit the width of corridors and we set up certain other definite requirements which he has to follow. We

have found that the comparative use of this measure results in a very definite check on extravagant design because its application at once discloses the existence of wasteful planning. [14 : 110]

In this study the interior cubatures of all rooms used for instructional purposes were taken from the lists of habitable cubatures prepared for each building. Educational cubature, therefore, includes all classroom, laboratory, shop, library, study hall, auditorium, and gymnasium cubature. The cost per cubic foot of educational cubature was based on this total.

Cost per square foot of floor area. Cost per square foot of floor area is easy to calculate. First the total area within the outside surfaces of a building is measured at each floor level. These areas are added to form the total number of square feet of floor area. Then the total cost of the building is divided by the total number of square feet of floor area. This gives the cost per square foot of floor area.

Cost per square foot of habitable floor area. Cost per square foot of habitable floor area is obtained by dividing the total cost of a building by the total number of square feet of floor area which can be occupied and used for school and its related work. In this study the interior floor areas of all habitable rooms and spaces were determined from the floor plans of the buildings. These floor areas were listed and totaled for each building.

Cost per square foot of educational floor area. Wiley [17 : 17] was among the first to suggest cost per square foot of educational floor area as a unit for comparing school building costs.

The first step in finding the cost per square foot of educational floor area of a building is to determine the floor areas of all rooms available for educational activities. The sum of these areas is the total educational floor area. If the total cost of the building is then divided by this total educational floor area, the result is the cost per square foot of educational floor area.

The terms "usable floor area" and "educational floor area" are not always uniformly interpreted. This is illustrated by the following quotation in which the term usable floor space is used to name what might be regarded as educational floor area.

In New Jersey the number of square feet of usable floor space is determined by adding the areas of all classrooms, auditoriums, gymnasiums, swimming pools, shower and locker rooms, offices, teachers' rooms, libraries, laboratories, toilet rooms and all special rooms. This does not include corridors, stairs, boiler-rooms, janitors' rooms, storerooms or cafeterias unless cafeterias are used as study rooms or for classroom purposes. Using this formula, comparisons can be readily made. [20:22]

In this study educational floor area includes the interior floor areas of all classrooms, laboratories, shops, libraries, study halls, auditoriums, and gymnasiums. Cost per square foot of educational floor area was based on this use of the term.

Cost per classroom. A generation ago, school buildings consisted of a number of uniformly large classrooms. The effect of an auditorium was created by rolling back folding doors between classrooms. A gymnasium was merely basement space which served also as a place in which children might assemble in cold or inclement weather. The relatively simple curriculum required little adaptation of school building design to varying instructional needs.

The cost of buildings was then frequently expressed in terms of cost per classroom. This unit cost was obtained by dividing the total cost by the number of classrooms in the building.

In this study the number of classrooms was taken from the floor plans of the buildings and checked with the lists of habitable rooms and spaces. Special classrooms, laboratories, shops, library rooms, and study halls were counted as classrooms. The cost per classroom was then determined for each building.

Cost per pupil. School building costs have also been compared on the basis of cost per pupil. This unit cost is determined by dividing the total cost by the number of pupils to be housed in the building.

For this study pupil capacity was defined as the total number of pupil stations in all classrooms, laboratories, shops, library rooms, and study halls.

Cost per pupil station. Cost per pupil station is a further attempt to express cost in terms of educational serviceability. The number of pupil stations in a building may be determined by counting the seats and desks in classrooms, chairs in the library, and other actual pupil stations; or the number of pupil stations may be calculated on the basis of empirically or experimentally established standards of area and volume for pupil stations of various types. The former method is subject to error when fewer than the optimum number of pupil stations are available in a room or when this number is exceeded because of overcrowding; the latter method results in more uniform estimates. The cost per pupil station is obtained by dividing the total cost by the total number of pupil stations.

In this study the number of pupil stations was determined by dividing the room floor areas by pupil station floor area standards used by the School Buildings and Grounds Division of the New York State Education Department. For ordinary classrooms and study halls this standard was 16.5 square feet per pupil. In certain special classrooms 25 square feet per pupil station was required. These special classrooms included rooms designated as: sewing, art, mechanical drawing, typing, bookkeeping, commercial, agriculture recitation, elementary science, music, dramatic arts, kindergarten, library, library-study hall, opportunity, and special class. For laboratories and similar rooms a standard of 35 square feet per pupil station was used. In this group were included rooms for: general science, advanced science, photography, physics, chemistry, and biology. In certain other rooms 50 square feet per pupil station was allowed. These rooms were indicated as: cooking, homemaking, home economics, model apartments, domestic science, foods laboratory, greenhouse, agriculture shop, general shop, vocational shop, manual training, and agriculture laboratory. A standard of 7 square feet per pupil station was used for auditoriums, 40 square feet for gymnasiums and combined auditorium-gymnasiums, 6 square feet for permanent bleacher sections, and 9 square feet for cafeterias.

Chapter V

Favorable and Unfavorable Criticisms of Units of Cost Other than Cost per Cubic Foot

Cost per classroom and special rooms. In 1914 Collins [9 : 19] found that reported costs of schools varied from $3,000 to $6,000 in cost per classroom. He found no record, however, of the proportion of corridors, cloak rooms, libraries or other spaces included in the prices.

In the years since 1914, school buildings have been designed with an increasing number of special rooms. The failure of cost per classroom to take account of these special rooms is reflected in criticisms by Baldwin, 1915; Betelle, 1922; Engelhardt and Engelhardt, 1930; and Halsey, 1934.

Baldwin [10 : 27] pointed out that the cost per classroom of a building containing twelve classrooms only is entirely different from the cost per classroom of a twelve-classroom building which also has an assembly hall, manual training room, cooking room, and sewing room.

Betelle contrasted the typical school building of an earlier day with those of 1922 as follows:

In earlier days, when a school consisted of four walls and a roof, divided on the interior into classrooms of equal size, the cost was given as a certain amount per classroom. . . . With the modern school building, containing an auditorium, gymnasium, locker and shower rooms, lunch room, large shops, study halls, and rooms of varying sizes, it can easily be seen that it is not possible to use the classroom as a unit of cost. [21 : 77]

In 1930 Engelhardt and Engelhardt wrote:

The classroom becomes less and less desirable as a building cost unit. This is particularly true as the plant facilities are extended

28

and an increasing number of special rooms are being provided for the elementary schools. [22 : 400]

Varying room requirements and cost per classroom. Wiley [17 : 17] pointed out that it is difficult to calculate the cost per classroom when room requirements vary as much as they do in a modern high school.

The variations in size of classrooms and the difference in standard dimensions for rooms were mentioned by Engelhardt and Engelhardt [22 : 400] as factors further limiting the value of the classroom unit.

Halsey emphasized the variations in size and number of accessory rooms:

If a school house contained nothing but classrooms, all with the same pupil capacity, then this [cost per classroom] would be a fair method of comparison. But school houses must have something more than classrooms. They must have all the accessory rooms, such as administrative offices, special activity rooms, toilet rooms, storerooms, and an auditorium and gymnasium with their accessories, which vary greatly in size and number in different buildings. In making a comparison by cost per classroom, all these important parts of the school house are ignored, and the method is a sort of rule of thumb with results too vague and indefinite for practical use. [18 : 21]

Modified cost per classroom unit. Moehlman criticized the cost per classroom unit and also the modified cost per classroom unit which he described thus:

The choice of this unit represented an earlier tendency to correlate instruction cost more intimately with plant function. Since the traditional and conventional organization was based largely on the teacher-classroom unit of administration, there was a certain amount of validity in its earlier use. Even under these early conditions, there were distinct variables in classroom size and ceiling height that made intra- and inter-community comparison of construction costs difficult. More recently, tendencies toward differentiated curriculums, followed by the development of specialized rooms, have increased the instability of the classroom as a unit of measure. Using approximate floor area as a base and considering auditoriums and gymnasiums as so many classrooms in accord with their size is not a valid procedure and may be very misleading.

Again, adding small, specialized units together and calling a group of them a classroom is scarcely worth while. The classroom as a measure of cost is rapidly becoming obsolete. [8 : 312]

Cost per square foot of floor area. Betelle [21 : 77-78] declared that cost per square foot of floor area is not satisfactory for comparing costs because different schools vary in types of rooms and in ceiling heights. Even in the same building rooms vary in height.

Cost per square foot of floor area and efficiency of planning. A building which is poorly planned for space utilization may appear more economical than a well-planned building if the comparison is made on the basis of cost per square foot. This is mentioned by Halsey:

A poorly planned building with a considerable amount of waste floor space or unavailable floor space or more floor space than is required to provide proper and sufficient accommodations for the school, will . . . be made to appear more economical than a building that is skillfully planned to provide a sufficient floor area to properly carry on the work of the school without any excess or unusable space. [18 : 20]

Wiley is of the same opinion:

It is difficult to make satisfactory comparisons on any total floor- or building-area basis when poor planning through an undue proportion of unusable areas will favorably influence the result. [17 : 17]

Cost per square foot of educational floor area. Wiley [17 : 17] suggests cost per square foot of educational floor area as a sound unit for comparing school building costs. This is essentially the basis used in New Jersey to compare school costs, although there it is called cost per square foot of "usable" floor space. [20 : 22]

Cost per pupil and special rooms. In 1914 Collins [9 : 19] found that reported costs of schools varied from $120 to $600 per pupil. He pointed out that some schools had large locker rooms, gymnasiums, domestic science departments, elaborate manual training facilities, libraries, wide corridors, reception rooms, auditoriums, and other spaces which must be housed but "do not have a definite pupil carrying capacity."

This fact is also mentioned by Donovan. He then calls attention to variations in the size and equipment of special rooms which affect cost per pupil:

> Furthermore, for comparison, this method [cost per pupil] is not reliable unless all the facts are known, for one school may have an assembly hall, playrooms, gymnasium, swimming-pool, etc., while another may have some of these rooms but not all of them, and they may be of smaller size and not as well equipped, or again they may not have any of them. [11 : 75]

Cost per pupil and type of structure. Type of structure is also a factor which should be considered in cost comparison on a per pupil basis. Collins wrote in 1914:

> Some prices may be for elaborate structures in the heart of a city where limited space requires putting up five stories and basement. The basement here would be only one-fifth of the building, while in a two-story building the basement may be the same size and one-third of the building contents. Yet the basement in both cases would be equally expensive and would be unproductive space as far as pupil rating is concerned. [9 : 19]

Variations in room sizes, number of special rooms, materials of construction, costs of labor, and other similarly important factors must be taken into account in interpreting costs per pupil, according to Engelhardt and Engelhardt. [22 : 400]

Cost per pupil and per pupil area standards. The number of square feet of floor space required by law for each pupil varies from one state to another. Morse and Anderson [20 : 22] point out that, since in New Jersey the standard is eighteen square feet of floor space per seat, while in many other states the standard is only fifteen square feet of floor space per seat, New Jersey school building costs cannot in fairness be compared with school building costs in other states on the basis of cost per pupil.

Cost per pupil and administration. Administration is a factor in determining the number of pupils who can be accommodated in a school building. This influences cost per pupil.

Morse and Anderson [20:22] point out that the maximum
pupil capacity of a school building varies according to the educational system used or the type of school housed. If the pla-
toon system is established, the maximum pupil capacity is
materially increased.

Wiley says:

It is difficult to determine the cost per pupil when the pupil
capacity may vary with different methods of administration, the
teacher load, or the number of periods per day. [17:17]

He further points out:

There is also the constant tendency to accept the enrollment as
pupil capacity, whereas the legal capacity as set up by state or other
codes is the real capacity. When enrollments are high, greatly in
excess of the legal capacity, as they often are, this enrollment is apt
to be considered not the overload it is but the actual pupil capacity.
[17:17]

Recognizing that the exact number of pupils for which a
building was planned is difficult to determine and that there
are few buildings, particularly high schools, which house the
number for which they were designed, Engelhardt and Engelhardt [22:399] came to the conclusion that cost per pupil station is probably better than cost per pupil for comparing educational service unit costs of school buildings.

Advantages of the cost per pupil station unit. Halsey
[18:21] declares that cost per pupil station is the most effective
unit to use for comparing school building costs. He asserts that
this unit cannot be juggled or distorted to make the cost of a
building appear other than it is. He considers cost per pupil
station the simplest of the cost units and one which has the
added advantage of being a measure of efficiency of planning.

Moehlman [8:316] considers the total number of pupil stations in a school building the absolute capacity of the building. The number of pupil stations, he points out, is a constant.
He concedes a certain amount of justification for the comparison of building erection or total costs on the basis of this
unit of instructional use.

Disadvantages of the cost per pupil station unit. Since cost per pupil station has not been widely discussed or applied, available criticism is limited.

Moehlman [8 : 316] does not consider the cost per pupil station unit entirely satisfactory. In his opinion, it does not give a true index of cost "since it assumes complete use of facilities and, therefore, ignores the difference between absolute and working capacity."

Chapter VI

Estimating the Cost of a
School Building

Approximate and detailed estimates. Estimates of the cost of a building are of two types: approximate and detailed. The latter are usually based on a quantity survey and involve the listing of all items of construction expense and of accurate unit costs for each item. Detailed estimates are used by contractors in preparing bids for proposed work. The making of these estimates is a very time-consuming process. Approximate estimates are made more quickly and are used in preliminary studies of a project.

There are numerous methods of making approximate estimates. All of these methods, however, consist of multiplying the number of units of size or capacity in the proposed structure by the known unit cost of a similar building already constructed. First, the size or capacity of the proposed building is expressed in terms of a convenient unit of measure. Then the approximate cost of the building is quickly determined by multiplying the number of units in terms of which the size or capacity of the proposed building was expressed by the corresponding unit cost of an existing similar building.

This study is concerned with an evaluation of the measures of building size or capacity used for making approximate estimates. The accuracy of such estimates depends, first, on the selection of a measure of building size or capacity which is closely associated with cost; second, on the choice of a building similar to the proposed building in major construction characteristics; and third, on the use of a unit cost which is truly representative of the cost of construction of the existing building. The more closely the measure of building size or capacity is related to total cost, the more nearly the proposed building resembles the existing building, and the more exactly the unit cost reflects the cost of construction of the existing building, the more accurate is the estimate of cost of the proposed building. Variations in prices of labor and materials must, of course, always be considered.

Measures of size or capacity of school buildings. The measures of size or capacity resulting from the application of the more common units of measure of school buildings are: total cubature, habitable cubature, educational cubature, total floor area, habitable floor area, educational floor area, number of classrooms, pupil capacity, and number of pupil stations. The accuracy of an estimate of cost of a proposed building made on the basis of one or more of these measures of building size or capacity depends, first, on the extent to which these measures are related to cost. In order to determine which of the nine measures of building size or capacity was most closely

Table 2

ZERO ORDER CORRELATION BETWEEN MEASURE OF BUILDING SIZE OR CAPACITY AND TOTAL COST

Measure	Zero Order Correlation	
	A	B
Total cubature *	.96	.98
Habitable cubature *	.95	.96
Educational cubature *	.92	.94
Total floor area *	.96	.97
Habitable floor area *	.95	.96
Educational floor area *	.91	.93
Number of classrooms *	.89	.90
Pupil capacity **	.92	.91
Number of pupil stations **	.83	.85

A = Total costs corrected for variations in wages and materials prices.
B = Total costs corrected for variations in wages and materials prices, plan types, type of construction, roof construction, and grade of interior finish.
 * Eight elementary schools, six secondary schools, and thirty-eight combined elementary and secondary schools.
 ** Thirty-eight combined elementary and secondary schools.

related to total cost, the New York State buildings included in this study were measured in terms of each, and these measures were then correlated with the total cost of the buildings. The cost of each building included the cost of general construction, heating and ventilating, plumbing, and electrical work. The total cost of each building was first corrected for variations in wages and materials prices. Then the costs were further corrected for variations due to general plan type, type of construction, roof construction, and grade of interior finish. The zero order correlations between the nine measures of building size or capacity and the total costs are given in Table 2.

Total cubature. Table 2 shows that, of the nine measures of building size or capacity studied, total cubature was most highly correlated with total cost. The zero order correlation between total cubature and total cost was .96 when the total costs were adjusted to eliminate the effects of variations in wages and materials prices only; the zero order correlation between total cubature and total cost was .98 when the total costs were further adjusted to eliminate the effects of variations in general plan type, type of construction, roof construction, and grade of interior finish.

Total floor area. It has been said that the use of square feet of floor area as a measure of building size or capacity is not sufficiently accurate for estimating the cost of a proposed building. The high correlations between total floor area and total construction cost, .96 and .97, tended to contradict this statement insofar as the buildings included in this study were concerned. Apparently, total floor area could be used in estimating the cost of a proposed building with almost as high a degree of accuracy as that attained through the use of total cubature.

Heterogeneity of the buildings as to size. The heterogeneity of the buildings as to size tended to make the correlations between the measures of building size or capacity and total cost very high and somewhat spurious. In order to investigate the relationships under more rigid conditions, a group of thirty buildings was chosen with a more restricted range in size. The new group of thirty buildings had a range in size less than one-

Table 3

ZERO ORDER CORRELATION BETWEEN MEASURE OF BUILDING SIZE OR
CAPACITY AND TOTAL COST—THIRTY SCHOOLS

*Cost Corrected for Variations in Wages and Materials Prices, Plan Types, Type
of Construction, Roof Construction, and Grade of Interior Finish*

Measure	Zero Order Correlation
Total cubature	.97
Habitable cubature	.92
Educational cubature	.86
Total floor area	.95
Habitable floor area	.94
Educational floor area	.87
Number of classrooms	.90
Pupil capacity	.86
Number of pupil stations	.72

third that of the group of fifty-two buildings. The larger group ranged from 124,000 cubic feet to 1,950,000 cubic feet; the smaller group had the more restricted range of 358,000 cubic feet to 950,000 cubic feet. The correlations between the nine measures of building size or capacity applied to this group of buildings and the total costs are reported in Table 3.

Similar results. The correlations obtained for the group of thirty buildings, restricted as to range in size, were not as high, but the relative positions of the nine measures of building size or capacity were approximately the same as before. Total cubature again was most highly correlated with total cost, the zero order correlation coefficient being .97. Total floor area again ranked second, with a correlation coefficient of .95.

Range in unit costs. When total cubature or any other measure is used as a basis for estimating the cost of a proposed school building, the total cubature or other measure of the building must be multiplied by a corresponding unit cost based on experience in the construction of other school buildings. The wide range in unit costs, as shown in Table 4, precludes the possibility of using a mean unit cost with much assurance of accuracy. Instead, the unit cost used must be representative of the cost of construction of school buildings similar to the one about to be built.

The school building to be erected must be similar in certain important characteristics to the school buildings whose known unit costs are to be used for estimating. If a proposed school building is similar in general plan, type of construction, roof construction, and interior finish to one or more buildings already built, and if it is to be erected under similar conditions insofar as prices of wages and materials are concerned, the cost of the proposed school building may be estimated with reasonable accuracy. If the proposed building is not similar to existing buildings in these respects, but if due allowances can be made for the lack of similarity, the cost of the new project may also be estimated with reasonable accuracy.

Table 4

RANGE IN UNIT COST

Cost Corrected for Variations in Wages and Materials Prices, Plan Type, Type of Construction, Roof Construction, and Grade of Interior Finish

Unit Cost	Low	High	Percentage of Difference ***
Cost per cubic foot *	$ .251	$ .416	65.7
Cost per cubic foot of habitable cubature *	.334	.678	103.0
Cost per cubic foot of educational cubature *	.442	1.115	161.3
Cost per square foot of floor area *..	4.11	8.22	100.0
Cost per square foot of habitable floor area *	4.60	9.24	100.9
Cost per square foot of educational floor area *.....................	6.66	18.09	171.6
Cost per classroom *...............	5,690.	18,910.	232.3
Cost per pupil **	242.	498.	105.8
Cost per pupil station **...........	98.	273.	178.6

* Eight elementary schools, six secondary schools, and thirty-eight combined elementary and secondary schools.
** Thirty-eight combined elementary and secondary schools.
*** The percentage of difference was obtained by dividing the difference between the high and low by the low value.

A further test. In order further to test the various measures of building size or capacity as bases for estimating the cost of a proposed building, several estimating situations were arranged. These were made as realistic as possible.

Construction patterns. The thirty-eight combined elementary and secondary school buildings were classified according to construction patterns. The buildings of one pattern were homogeneous in each of several construction characteristics: type of roof, type of construction, interior finish materials, and number of floors above the basement. Type of roof was divided into two categories, type of construction into three, interior finish materials into three, and number of floors into two. These categories were the same as those used by Engelhardt, Jr. in his study. [6] This plan resulted in the classification of the buildings according to fourteen patterns.

Plan type. The buildings in the five patterns represented by only one building each were eliminated. The buildings classified according to each of the nine remaining patterns were then examined for similarity of plan type. Any building which was not similar in plan type to the other buildings of its pattern group was also eliminated. In one case a pattern group of six buildings was subdivided into three pairs on the basis of plan type. The final classification left one group of six buildings, one group of three buildings, and eight pairs of buildings.

Estimating the total costs. It was decided to estimate the cost of each building in the group of six by multiplying each measure applied to this building by the corresponding median unit costs of the other five buildings. The cost of each building in the group of three was similarly estimated by multiplying each measure applied to this building by the corresponding average unit costs of the other two buildings. The cost of each building of the eight pairs of buildings was estimated by multiplying each measure applied to the building by the corresponding unit costs of the building with which it was paired. These estimated total costs were then compared with the actual total costs and the percentages of difference were determined.

Difference between actual and estimated costs. Table 5

Table 5

DIFFERENCE BETWEEN ACTUAL TOTAL CONSTRUCTION COST
AND ESTIMATED TOTAL CONSTRUCTION COST

Twenty-five Combined Elementary and Secondary Schools

Measure	Average * Percentage of Difference
Total cubature	8.2
Habitable cubature	13.1
Educational cubature	16.4
Total floor area	9.9
Habitable floor area	12.3
Educational floor area	13.2
Number of classrooms	12.1
Pupil capacity	19.7
Number of pupil stations	29.5

* The sign of a difference was not considered.

shows the average percentage of difference between actual total construction costs and estimated total construction costs based on the nine measures of building size or capacity. Total cubature proved to be the best basis for estimating the cost of the twenty-five buildings. Its average percentage of difference between actual and estimated cost, 8.2, was lowest of the nine. Total floor area, with an average percentage of difference of 9.9, was next best. The sign of a difference was not considered.

Summary. Total cubature proved to be the best measure of building size or capacity to use as a basis for estimating the cost of a proposed building. Total cubature had the highest correlation with total cost of construction. The average percentage of difference between actual and estimated total cost of construction based on total cubature was 8.2.

Total floor area was found to be the second best measure of building size or capacity to use as a basis for estimating the cost of a proposed building. Total floor area had the second highest correlation with total cost of construction. The average percentage of difference between actual and estimated total cost of construction based on total floor area was 9.9.

Chapter VII

Unit Costs in Relation to Designing and Planning of School Buildings

Two examples of this type of unit. Some of the units of cost report school building costs in such a way that good designing and skillful planning appear to advantage. Two examples are cost per cubic foot of habitable cubature and cost per square foot of habitable floor area.

A number of statements have been made regarding the units of cost and their relationship to efficiency of designing and planning. Among them appear the following:

1. Cost per cubic foot gives no indication of plan efficiency. [8:313]

2. The more expansive and loose the design, the lower will be the cost per cubic foot and the higher the cost per pupil. [15:159] Conversely, the more compact the plan, the higher will be the cost per cubic foot and the lower the cost per pupil. [15:159]

3. Cost per cubic foot of educational cubature reveals wasteful planning. [14:110]

4. Cost per pupil station is a measure of efficiency of plan. [18:21]

Purposes of this portion of the study. The purposes of this portion of the study were: (1) to test these statements regarding the units of cost and (2) to determine which of the units of cost best reflects efficiency of designing and planning.

Efficiency of designing and planning. For purposes of this study, a building was considered efficiently designed and planned to the extent that its size, shape, and height permitted economy of construction and to the extent that its internal arrangement provided an optimum of habitable space.

Small buildings are relatively expensive to build if the same type of construction is used in them as in large buildings. [12:40] [18:20-21]

Buildings which are irregular in shape require more exterior wall to enclose a given amount of cubature than do square, compact buildings. This additional exterior wall increases the relative cost of construction.

If shape is held constant, the amount of exterior wall required to enclose a unit of cubature varies inversely with size of building. A small building requires more exterior wall per unit of cubature enclosed than a large building.

Buildings which are spread out require more extensive piping for their heating and ventilating systems than compact structures. [6:60]

Small buildings, low buildings, and buildings which are spread out require more roof per unit of cubature.

One-story buildings are relatively more expensive to build than two-story and three-story buildings of similar type of construction.

Ratio of perimeter to ground area. The ratio of the number of linear feet of perimeter of a building to the number of square feet of ground area covered by a building was used as a

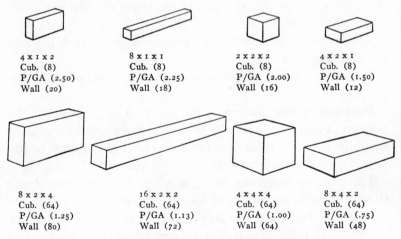

4 X 1 X 2
Cub. (8)
P/GA (2.50)
Wall (20)

8 X 1 X 1
Cub. (8)
P/GA (2.25)
Wall (18)

2 X 2 X 2
Cub. (8)
P/GA (2.00)
Wall (16)

4 X 2 X 1
Cub. (8)
P/GA (1.50)
Wall (12)

8 X 2 X 4
Cub. (64)
P/GA (1.25)
Wall (80)

16 X 2 X 2
Cub. (64)
P/GA (1.13)
Wall (72)

4 X 4 X 4
Cub. (64)
P/GA (1.00)
Wall (64)

8 X 4 X 2
Cub. (64)
P/GA (.75)
Wall (48)

FIG. 1. Ratio of Perimeter to Ground Area of Building

measure of size and shape of a building, indicating the amount of exterior wall required to enclose a given amount of cubature. As this ratio decreases, the amount of wall required to enclose a given amount of cubature decreases. Therefore, efficiency of designing and planning increases.

This ratio decreases, if shape is held constant and size is increased, or, if size is held constant and shape is varied so that less wall per unit of cubature is required. The simplified building shapes in Fig. 1 show how changes in size and shape affect the ratio of perimeter to ground area.

Ratio of perimeter to total cubature. The ratio of the number of linear feet of perimeter of a building to the total cubature of the building was used as a measure of the size and shape of a building, indicating the degree to which a building is spread out. As this ratio decreases, a building becomes larger or less spread out. Therefore, efficiency of designing and planning increases.

This ratio decreases, if shape is held constant and size is increased, or, if size is held constant and shape is varied so that the building has less perimeter. The simplified building shapes in Figure 2 show how changes in size and shape affect the ratio of perimeter to total cubature.

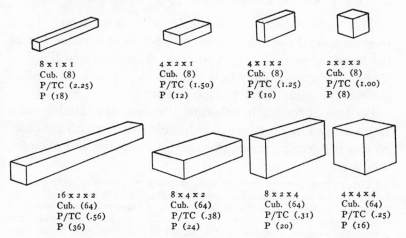

8 x 1 x 1
Cub. (8)
P/TC (2.25)
P (18)

4 x 2 x 1
Cub. (8)
P/TC (1.50)
P (12)

4 x 1 x 2
Cub. (8)
P/TC (1.25)
P (10)

2 x 2 x 2
Cub. (8)
P/TC (1.00)
P (8)

16 x 2 x 2
Cub. (64)
P/TC (.56)
P (36)

8 x 4 x 2
Cub. (64)
P/TC (.38)
P (24)

8 x 2 x 4
Cub. (64)
P/TC (.31)
P (20)

4 x 4 x 4
Cub. (64)
P/TC (.25)
P (16)

Fig. 2. Ratio of Perimeter to Total Cubature of Building

Ratio of ground area to total cubature. The ratio of the number of square feet of ground area covered by a building to the total cubature of the building was used as a measure of the height of a building.[1] This ratio also indicates the amount of roof required to cover a given amount of cubature. As this ratio decreases, height increases and amount of roof required to cover a given amount of cubature decreases. Therefore, efficiency of designing and planning increases.

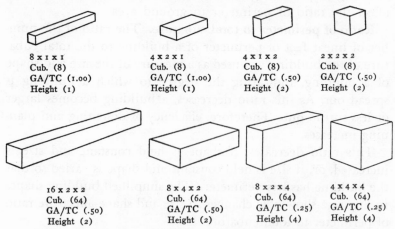

8 x 1 x 1
Cub. (8)
GA/TC (1.00)
Height (1)

4 x 2 x 1
Cub. (8)
GA/TC (1.00)
Height (1)

4 x 1 x 2
Cub. (8)
GA/TC (.50)
Height (2)

2 x 2 x 2
Cub. (8)
GA/TC (.50)
Height (2)

16 x 2 x 2
Cub. (64)
GA/TC (.50)
Height (2)

8 x 4 x 2
Cub. (64)
GA/TC (.50)
Height (2)

8 x 2 x 4
Cub. (64)
GA/TC (.25)
Height (4)

4 x 4 x 4
Cub. (64)
GA/TC (.25)
Height (4)

FIG. 3. Ratio of Ground Area to Total Cubature of Building

This ratio decreases, if shape is held constant and size is increased, or, if size is held constant and shape is varied so that the building covers less ground area. The simplified building shapes in Figure 3 show how changes in size and shape affect the ratio of ground area to total cubature.

Per cent of habitable cubature. Per cent of habitable cubature was used as a measure of habitable space in each building. As this per cent increases, efficiency of designing and planning increases.

[1] The ratio of ground area to total cubature was used as a measure of height because many of the buildings were designed with sections of varying height. A building, for example, might have a three-story main section, a two-story wing projecting to the rear, and a story-and-a-half auditorium and gymnasium wing on either side. The height of this type of building could not be expressed directly. The ratio of ground area to total cubature was, therefore, used as a measure of the relative flatness of the buildings.

Assumptions relative to efficiency of designing and planning. The plans and specifications for these buildings were approved by the School Buildings and Grounds Division of the New York State Education Department. Prior to approval they had been carefully checked by a member of the Division staff. It was assumed, therefore, that the placement of rooms in the building and other internal arrangement of spaces were efficiently planned. This phase of efficiency of designing and planning is important, but it is also an aspect of school building construction which has received much attention from architects and educators. The broad aspects of efficiency of designing and planning emphasized in this study have received less consideration in spite of the fact that they account for large differences in cost of construction. [6:87]

Procedure. Unit costs, calculated on the basis of the various measures of building size or capacity, were correlated with the four measures of efficiency of designing and planning: (1) ratio of perimeter of a building to ground area covered by the building, (2) ratio of perimeter of a building to total cubature of the building, (3) ratio of ground area covered by a building to total cubature of the building, and (4) per cent of habitable cubature in a building.

Unit costs. The unit costs correlated with the three ratios were based on total construction costs which had been corrected to eliminate the effects of variation in wages and materials prices, type of construction, roof construction, and grade of interior finish of the buildings. The unit costs correlated with per cent of habitable cubature were based on total construction costs which had been corrected to eliminate the effect of each of the above variables and had also been corrected for variations related to the general plan type of the buildings. [6]

Correlations. The zero order correlation coefficients for the relationship between unit cost and ratio of perimeter to ground area are shown in Table 6, Column A; those between unit cost and ratio of perimeter to total cubature, in Table 6, Column B; those between unit cost and ratio of ground area to total cubature, in Table 6, Column C; and those between unit cost

Table 6

ZERO ORDER CORRELATION BETWEEN UNIT COST AND
MEASURE OF SIZE AND SHAPE

Cost Corrected for Variations in Wages and Materials Prices, Type of Construction, Roof Construction, and Grade of Interior Finish

Unit Cost	Zero Order Correlation			Multiple Correlation
	A	B	C	
Cost per cubic foot *	.58	.58	.32	.62
Cost per cubic foot of habitable cubature *	.65	.60	.28	.68
Cost per cubic foot of educational cubature *	.56	.43	.06	.64
Cost per square foot of floor area *	.56	.53	.25	.60
Cost per square foot of habitable floor area *	.53	.49	.21	.56
Cost per square foot of educational floor area *	.38	.26	—.05	.49
Cost per classroom *	.31	.26	—.002	.42
Cost per pupil **	—.09	—.32	—.42	.45
Cost per pupil station **	.19	.19	.07	.21

A = Ratio of perimeter of building to ground area of building.
B = Ratio of perimeter of building to total cubature of building.
C = Ratio of ground area of building to total cubature of building.
 * Eight elementary schools, six secondary schools, and thirty-eight combined elementary and secondary schools.
** Thirty-eight combined elementary and secondary schools.

and per cent of habitable cubature, in Table 7. The multiple correlation coefficients for the relationship between unit cost and the three ratios used as measures of efficiency of designing and planning affecting the shape of a building are also given in Table 6.

Cost per cubic foot. Compared with the other eight unit costs studied, cost per cubic foot was found to have a relatively high positive correlation with each of the three ratios: perimeter to ground area, perimeter to total cubature, and ground area to total cubature. Cost per cubic foot was found, therefore, to have a relatively high inverse correlation with efficiency of designing and planning insofar as this designing and

Table 7

ZERO ORDER CORRELATION BETWEEN UNIT COST AND PER CENT
OF HABITABLE CUBATURE

*Cost Corrected for Variations in Wages and Materials Prices, Plan Type, Type
of Construction, Roof Construction, and Grade of Interior Finish*

Unit Cost	Zero Order Correlation
Cost per cubic foot *	—.09
Cost per cubic foot of habitable cubature *	—.72
Cost per cubic foot of educational cubature *	—.74
Cost per square foot of floor area *	—.60
Cost per square foot of habitable floor area *	—.62
Cost per square foot of educational floor area *	—.59
Cost per classroom *	—.57
Cost per pupil **	—.54
Cost per pupil station **	—.52

* Eight elementary schools, six secondary schools, and thirty-eight combined
  elementary and secondary schools.
** Thirty-eight combined elementary and secondary schools.

planning affect the size and shape of a building. This is contrary to expressed opinion. [8:313] Also contradicted was the opinion [15:159] that the more expensive and loose the design, the lower the cost per cubic foot, and, conversely, the more compact the plan, the higher the cost per cubic foot. Cost per cubic foot decreased as amount of wall required to enclose a given amount of cubature decreased, as the buildings became larger and less spread out, and as the buildings became higher. The correlation of cost per cubic foot with ratio of perimeter to ground area was .58; with ratio of perimeter to total cubature, .58; and with ratio of ground area to total cubature, .32. The multiple correlation between cost per cubic foot and the three ratios was .62.

No significant relationship was found between cost per cubic foot and per cent of habitable cubature. The zero order correlation coefficient indicating this relationship was —.09. This low coefficient tends to support the opinion that cost per cubic foot gives no indication of efficiency of planning. [8:313]

Cost per cubic foot was found to be inversely related to efficiency of designing and planning insofar as this affects the size and shape of a building, but not significantly related to efficiency of designing and planning insofar as this affects the amount of habitable cubature in a building. The statement that cost per cubic foot gives no indication of plan efficiency [8 : 313] was, therefore, partly supported and partly contradicted.

Cost per cubic foot of habitable cubature. Cost per cubic foot of habitable cubature was also found significantly correlated with the three ratios used as measures of efficiency of designing and planning affecting the size and shape of a building. Cost per cubic foot of habitable cubature had the highest correlation with ratio of perimeter to ground area and with ratio of perimeter to total cubature, .65 and .60, respectively. It was found that the less exterior wall required to enclose a given amount of cubature, the larger and less spread out the building, and the higher the building, the lower the cost per cubic foot of habitable cubature. The multiple correlation between cost per cubic foot of habitable cubature and the three ratios was .68.

The zero order correlation coefficient expressing the relationship between cost per cubic foot of habitable cubature and per cent of habitable cubature was —.72. A correlation at least as high as this was anticipated. The contrast between cost per cubic foot and cost per cubic foot of habitable cubature should, however, be noted. The former had a correlation coefficient of —.09 and the latter a coefficient of —.72 when correlated with per cent of habitable cubature. Cost per cubic foot of habitable cubature was found more highly related in a negative sense to efficiency of designing and planning than was cost per cubic foot.

Cost per cubic foot of educational cubature. Cost per cubic foot of educational cubature had the highest correlation with per cent of habitable cubature, —.74. It was also significantly correlated with ratio of perimeter to ground area and with ratio of perimeter to total cubature, .56 and .43 respectively.

It was not significantly correlated with ratio of ground area to total cubature, .06.

The claim that comparisons of costs of school buildings, when made on the basis of cost per cubic foot of educational cubature, reveal wasteful planning [14 : 110] was found justified. The higher the per cent of habitable cubature, the less wall required to enclose a given amount of cubature, and the larger and less spread out the building, the lower the cost per cubic foot of educational cubature.

Cost per pupil. It has been maintained that the more expansive and loose the design, the higher the cost per pupil, and, conversely, the more compact the plan, the lower the cost per pupil. [15 : 159] This can be neither affirmed nor denied on the basis of the evidence made available through this study. Compared with the correlations between the other unit costs and per cent of habitable cubature, the correlation between cost per pupil and per cent of habitable cubature was relatively low, —.54. Moreover, no significant relationship was found to exist between cost per pupil and ratio of perimeter to ground area and ratio of perimeter to total cubature. The correlation coefficients, —.09 and —.32 respectively, might have been the result only of chance. The correlation between cost per pupil and the ratio of ground area to total cubature, —.42, is statistically significant. In view of the lack of supporting evidence in the other two correlations, however, it did not seem justifiable to conclude that the relationship between cost per pupil and efficiency of designing and planning indicated in the opinion that the more expansive and loose the design, the higher the cost per pupil [15 : 159] does not exist.

Cost per pupil station. It has been asserted that cost per pupil station is a desirable unit of cost for comparing school building costs because it is a measure of efficiency of planning. [18 : 21] No support for this opinion was found. Compared with the correlations between the other unit costs and the per cent of habitable cubature, the correlation between cost per pupil station and per cent of habitable cubature was relatively low, —.52. The correlations between cost per pupil station and the three ratios used as measures of efficiency of designing and planning affecting the size and shape of a building were not statistically significant.

Partial correlations. In order to determine how much of the relationship between unit costs and measures of efficiency of designing and planning was independent of variations in size of the buildings, partial correlations were obtained. These partial correlations indicated the degree of association between unit costs and efficiency of designing and planning which is independent of building size. The partial correlation coefficients for the relationship between unit cost and ratio of perimeter to ground area independent of size are shown in Table 8, Column A; those between unit cost and ratio of perimeter to total cubature independent of size, in Table 8, Column B; those between unit cost and ratio of ground area to total cuba-

Table 8

PARTIAL CORRELATION BETWEEN UNIT COST AND MEASURE OF
SIZE AND SHAPE INDEPENDENT OF SIZE

*Cost Corrected for Variations in Wages and Materials Prices, Type of
Construction, Roof Construction, and Grade of Interior Finish*

Unit Cost	Partial Correlation		
	A	B	C
Cost per cubic foot *	.49	.49	.18
Cost per cubic foot of habitable cubature *	.59	.51	.13
Cost per cubic foot of educational cubature *	.45	.27	—.11
Cost per square foot of floor area *	.51	.46	.13
Cost per square foot of habitable floor area *	.48	.42	.09
Cost per square foot of educational floor area *	.31	.14	—.17
Cost per classroom *	.21	.15	—.11
Cost per pupil **	—.21	—.51	—.50
Cost per pupil station **	—.18	—.26	—.19

A = Ratio of perimeter of building to ground area of building.
B = Ratio of perimeter of building to total cubature of building.
C = Ratio of ground area of building to total cubature of building.
 * Eight elementary schools, six secondary schools, and thirty-eight combined elementary and secondary schools.
** Thirty-eight combined elementary and secondary schools.

ture independent of size, in Table 8, Column C; and those between unit cost and per cent of habitable cubature independent of size, in Table 9.

Elimination of the influence of size of buildings is reflected in the differences between the partial correlations and the zero order correlations. These differences, however, are not inordinate. Shape of building is the significant factor in determining the efficiency ratios: perimeter to ground area, perimeter to total cubature, and ground area to total cubature. Size of building is of secondary importance. Per cent of habitable cubature is even more independent of size of building. The relative degrees of correlation of the unit costs were little changed. The general conclusions based on the zero order correlations were, therefore, sustained.

Table 9

PARTIAL CORRELATION BETWEEN UNIT COST AND PER CENT OF HABITABLE CUBATURE INDEPENDENT OF SIZE

Cost Corrected for Variations in Wages and Materials Prices, Plan Type, Type of Construction, Roof Construction, and Grade of Interior Finish

Unit Cost	Partial Correlation
Cost per cubic foot *	—.09
Cost per cubic foot of habitable cubature *	—.71
Cost per cubic foot of educational cubature *	—.72
Cost per square foot of floor area *	—.59
Cost per square foot of habitable floor area *	—.62
Cost per square foot of educational floor area *	—.59
Cost per classroom *	—.57
Cost per pupil **	—.55
Cost per pupil station **	—.57

* Eight elementary schools, six secondary schools, and thirty-eight combined elementary and secondary schools.
** Thirty-eight combined elementary and secondary schools.

Summary. Contrary to expressed opinion, cost per cubic foot was found to have a relatively high inverse correlation with efficiency of designing and planning insofar as designing and planning affect the size and shape of a building. Cost per cubic foot decreased as amount of wall required to enclose a given amount of cubature decreased, as the buildings became larger or less spread out, and as the buildings became higher. In other words, cost per cubic foot decreased as efficiency of designing and planning affecting the size and shape of a building increased. On the other hand, no significant relationship was found between cost per cubic foot and per cent of habitable cubature. This tends to support the opinion that cost per cubic foot gives no indication of efficiency of planning. This opinion was, therefore, partly supported and partly contradicted.

The claim that comparisons of costs of school buildings, when made on the basis of cost per cubic foot of educational cubature, reveal wasteful planning was found to be justified. The higher the per cent of habitable cubature, the less wall required to enclose a given amount of cubature, and the larger or less spread out the building, the lower the cost per cubic foot of educational cubature.

This study adduced no conclusive evidence regarding a relationship between cost per pupil and efficiency of designing and planning.

No support was found for the contention that cost per pupil station is a measure of efficiency of planning.

Cost per cubic foot of habitable cubature had the highest correlation with ratio of perimeter to ground area and with ratio of perimeter to total cubature.

Cost per cubic foot of habitable cubature was found more highly related in a negative sense to efficiency of designing and planning than any of the other eight units of cost. As efficiency of designing and planning increased, cost per cubic foot of habitable cubature decreased.

Chapter VIII

Unit Costs in Relation to Educational Serviceability of School Buildings

Three examples of this type of unit. Several of the units make it possible to report school building costs in such a way that buildings with greater educational serviceability appear to advantage. Three examples of this type of unit are: cost per cubic foot of educational cubature, cost per square foot of educational floor area, and cost per pupil station.

A number of statements have been made regarding the units of cost and their relationship to educational serviceability. Among these are:

1. Cost per cubic foot does not serve as a measure of the "educational value" of a building. [19:60] Cost per cubic foot does not indicate any relation of structure to use. [8:311]

2. Low cost per cubic foot may, in certain instances, be associated with high cost per pupil. [16:107]

Purposes of this portion of the study. The purposes of this portion of the study were: (1) to test these statements and (2) to determine which of the units are most closely related to measures of the educational serviceability of school buildings.

Educational serviceability. For purposes of this study, a building was considered to have educational serviceability to the extent that its internal arrangement provided an optimum of space for instructional purposes in the building.

Per cent of educational cubature and per cent of educational floor area were used as measures of educational space in each building. As these per cents increase, educational serviceability increases.

Assumptions relative to educational serviceability. The School Buildings and Grounds Division of the New York State

53

Education Department approved the plans and specifications for the buildings studied. The educational needs of each community were studied as a preliminary to planning. It was assumed, therefore, that the buildings studied were designed to provide adequate educational service facilities to carry on a program of education acceptable to the New York State Education Department.

Procedure. Unit costs calculated on the basis of the various measures of building size or capacity were correlated with two measures of educational serviceability: (1) per cent of educational cubature and (2) per cent of educational floor area.

The part of the Strayer-Engelhardt Score Card for High School Buildings [23] dealing with special rooms was applied to each of the combined elementary and secondary school buildings. This provided another measure of educational serviceability. Correlations between the nine measures of building size or capacity and the Score Card ratings showed the extent to which the nine measures of building size or capacity also measured the educational serviceability of the buildings.

Correlations. The zero order correlation coefficients for the relationship between unit cost and per cent of educational cubature are shown in Table 10, Column A; those between unit cost and per cent of educational floor area, in Table 10, Column B; and those between measure of building size or capacity and Score Card rating in Table 11. The multiple correlation coefficients for the relationship between unit cost and per cent of educational cubature and per cent of educational floor area are also given in Table 10.

Cost per cubic foot. It has been said that cost per cubic foot does not serve as a measure of the "educational value" of a building. [19:60] Cost per cubic foot does not indicate any relation of structure to use. [8:311]

In conformity with these opinions, no significant correlation was found between cost per cubic foot and per cent of educational cubature or between cost per cubic foot and per cent of educational floor area. Moreover, compared with the correlation between the other measures of building size or capacity

Table 10

ZERO ORDER CORRELATION BETWEEN UNIT COST AND PER CENT OF EDUCA-
TIONAL CUBATURE AND PER CENT OF EDUCATIONAL FLOOR AREA

*Cost Corrected for Variations in Wages and Materials Prices, Plan Type, Type
of Construction, Roof Construction, and Grade of Interior Finish*

Unit Cost	Zero Order Correlation		Multiple Correlation
	A	B	
Cost per cubic foot *	—.07	—.10	.10
Cost per cubic foot of habitable cubature *	—.60	—.25	.65
Cost per cubic foot of educational cubature *	—.83	—.60	.83
Cost per square foot of floor area *	—.47	—.18	.52
Cost per square foot of habitable floor area *	—.50	—.27	.51
Cost per square foot of educational floor area *	—.73	—.71	.78
Cost per classroom *	—.65	—.59	.68
Cost per pupil **	—.57	—.42	.57
Cost per pupil station **	—.64	—.64	.69

A = Per cent of educational cubature.
B = Per cent of educational floor area.
 * Eight elementary schools, six secondary schools, and thirty-eight combined
elementary and secondary schools.
** Thirty-eight combined elementary and secondary schools.

Table 11

ZERO ORDER CORRELATION BETWEEN MEASURE OF BUILDING SIZE
OR CAPACITY AND SCORE CARD RATING

Thirty-eight Combined Elementary and Secondary Schools

Measure	Zero Order Correlation
Total cubature	.83
Habitable cubature	.87
Educational cubature	.88
Total floor area	.85
Habitable floor area	.86
Educational floor area	.90
Number of classrooms	.84
Pupil capacity	.79
Number of pupil stations	.92

and Score Card rating, the correlation between total cubature and Score Card rating was relatively low, indicating that total cubature is a relatively poor measure of the educational serviceability of a school building.

Cost per cubic foot of educational cubature. Cost per cubic foot of educational cubature was found to be a good unit of cost on the basis of relationship to educational serviceability of school buildings. Cost per cubic foot of educational cubature had the highest inverse correlation with per cent of educational cubature, —.83, and a relatively high inverse correlation with per cent of educational floor area, —.60. Cost per cubic foot of educational cubature tended to decrease as per cents of educational cubature and educational floor area increased.

The multiple correlation between cost per cubic foot of educational cubature and per cent of educational cubature and per cent of educational floor area was .83.

Educational cubature is also a good measure of the educational serviceability of a school building. This is shown by the correlation coefficient of .88 for the relationship between educational cubature and Score Card rating.

Cost per square foot of educational floor area. Cost per square foot of educational floor area was also found to be a good unit of cost from the standpoint of reflecting the educational serviceability of school buildings. Cost per square foot of educational floor area had the highest inverse correlation with per cent of educational floor area, —.71, and the second highest inverse correlation with per cent of educational cubature, —.73. As per cent of educational floor area and per cent of educational cubature increased, cost per square foot of educational floor area tended to decrease.

The multiple correlation between cost per square foot of educational floor area and per cent of educational cubature and per cent of educational floor area was .78.

Educational floor area also had the second highest correlation with Score Card rating, .90, indicating that the number of square feet of educational floor area is a good measure of the educational serviceability of a school building.

Cost per pupil station. Number of pupil stations had the highest correlation with Score Card rating, .92.

Cost per pupil station was also found to be significantly related in a negative sense to per cent of educational cubature and per cent of educational floor area. The correlation coefficient in each case was —.64, and the multiple correlation coefficient was .69. Cost per pupil station tended to decrease as per cent of educational cubature and per cent of educational floor area increased.

Cost per pupil and cost per cubic foot. It has been pointed out [16 : 107] that low cost per cubic foot may, in certain instances, be associated with high cost per pupil. The possibility of this will, of course, always be present. In the buildings studied, however, there was no general tendency for low cost per cubic foot to be associated with high cost per pupil. The correlation coefficient expressing the relationship between these two unit costs was .16.

Table 12

PARTIAL CORRELATION BETWEEN UNIT COST AND PER CENT OF
EDUCATIONAL CUBATURE AND PER CENT OF EDUCATIONAL
FLOOR AREA INDEPENDENT OF SIZE OF BUILDING

Unit Cost	Partial Correlation	
	A	B
Cost per cubic foot *	—.09	—.15
Cost per cubic foot of habitable cubature *	—.61	—.32
Cost per cubic foot of educational cubature *	—.83	—.64
Cost per square foot of floor area *	—.47	—.23
Cost per square foot of habitable floor area *	—.50	—.31
Cost per square foot of educational floor area *	—.73	—.72
Cost per classroom *	—.65	—.60
Cost per pupil **	—.57	—.44
Cost per pupil station **	—.69	—.66

A = Per cent of educational cubature.
B = Per cent of educational floor area.
  * Eight elementary schools, six secondary schools, and thirty-eight combined elementary and secondary schools.
** Thirty-eight combined elementary and secondary schools.

Partial correlations. In order to determine how much of the relationship between the unit costs and the measures of educational serviceability was independent of variations in the size of the buildings, partial correlations were obtained. The partial correlation coefficients for the relationship between unit cost and per cent of educational cubature independent of size of building are shown in Table 12, Column A; and those between unit cost and per cent of educational floor area independent of size of building in Table 12, Column B.

Elimination of the influence of size of building had little effect upon the correlations between unit costs and per cent of educational cubature and per cent of educational floor area. The general conclusions based on the zero order correlations were sustained.

Summary. The opinion that cost per cubic foot gives no indication of the educational serviceability of a school building was confirmed by this study.

There was no general tendency for low cost per cubic foot to be associated with high cost per pupil.

Cost per cubic foot of educational cubature, cost per square foot of educational floor area, and cost per pupil station were found to be good units of cost from the standpoint of reflecting the educational serviceability of school buildings.

Number of pupil stations was found to be most highly related to Score Card rating of the buildings.

Chapter IX

Cost per Weighted Pupil Station, A New Unit

Introduction. Total cubature is the best measure of building size or capacity to use in estimating the cost of a proposed school building. Cost per cubic foot, however, is a very unsatisfactory unit to use for comparing school building costs. A building which appears inexpensive because it has a low cost per cubic foot may really be expensive because only a relatively small percentage of its cubature is available for use. Cost per cubic foot of habitable cubature is not subject to this criticism. Cost per cubic foot of habitable cubature is the best unit of cost from the standpoint of reflecting differences in efficiency of designing and planning of school buildings. Cost per cubic foot of educational cubature, cost per square foot of educational floor area, and cost per pupil station are the best units of cost from the standpoint of reflecting differences in educational serviceability of school buildings. None of the nine units studied so far is entirely satisfactory for every purpose and from every point of view.

A weighted pupil station unit. For years N. L. Engelhardt has believed that a weighted pupil station unit could be developed which would make school building costs truly comparable and which would be understood by architects and by laymen. The fact that cost per cubic foot of educational cubature, cost per square foot of educational floor area, and cost per pupil station were found to be good units of cost from the standpoint of reflecting differences in educational serviceability of school buildings suggested the possibility of combining these units in a weighted pupil station unit. Such a unit would probably not be superior to cost per cubic foot of habitable cuba-

59

ture in cost comparisons related to the efficiency of designing and planning of school buildings, but a weighted pupil station unit might prove useful in cost comparisons related to the educational serviceability of school buildings. Even if the number of weighted pupil stations in a building did not prove to be as good a basis for estimating the cost of a proposed building as total cubature, the new unit would still be useful. Estimates based on number of weighted pupil stations could be made even before preliminary plans had been drawn. A weighted pupil station unit would permit the estimating of costs from a statement of need before plans were drawn. The weighted pupil station unit could, of course, also be applied after preliminary plans had been drawn. Even if the number of weighted pupil stations in a building is not as good a basis for estimating the cost of a proposed building as total cubature, estimates of cost made in this way would serve for checking a cost estimate based on total cubature.

Weighting in terms of area and cubature. The number of pupil stations having been determined through the use of floor area standards, the next step was to weight these pupil stations according to the different cubatures required for the various types of pupil station.

The ceiling height of classrooms in the buildings studied was, almost without exception, 12 feet. Consequently, in ordinary classrooms having 16.5 square feet per pupil station, the cubature per pupil station was 198 cubic feet. This cubature per pupil station in an ordinary classroom was taken as the base for the weighting in terms of cubature and was given a weighted pupil station value of 1.00. In classrooms having 25 square feet per pupil station the cubature per pupil station was 300 cubic feet. The ratio of cubature per pupil station in this type of room to cubature per pupil station in an ordinary classroom gave a weighted pupil station equivalent of a classroom station having 25 square feet per pupil. Each pupil station in a room having 25 square feet per pupil station was given a weighted pupil station value of 1.52. In a similar manner the cubature per pupil station in laboratories, 420 cubic feet, divided by the base cubature of 198 cubic feet per pupil station in ordinary classrooms gave a weighted pupil station equivalent of 2.12 for laboratory pupil stations. The weighted pupil station equivalent for pupil stations requiring 50 square feet of floor area per pupil station was similarly found to be 3.03.

There was no standard height for auditoriums, gymnasiums, auditorium-gymnasiums, bleachers, and cafeterias. The average cubature per pupil station for these facilities was therefore ascertained for the group of buildings. Table 13 shows that a total of 1,373,652 cubic feet was provided for 7,355 auditorium pupil stations. This included the cubature for the stage. The stage cubature was not considered in calculating the number of pupil stations in the auditorium. The mean cubature per auditorium pupil station was 186.76 cubic feet. Similarly it was found that the mean cubature per gymnasium pupil station was 937.70 cubic feet; per auditorium-gymnasium pupil station, 1,115.56 cubic feet; per bleacher pupil station, 97.81 cubic feet; and per cafeteria pupil station, 134.18 cubic feet.

The average cubature per auditorium pupil station, 186.76, was then divided by 198, the cubature required for an ordinary classroom pupil station. The resulting quotient, .94, was the weighted pupil station equivalent of an auditorium pupil station. Similarly the remaining weighted pupil station equivalents were found to be: gymnasium, 4.74; auditorium-gymnasium, 5.63; bleacher, .49; and cafeteria, .68.

Table 13

MEAN CUBATURE PER PUPIL STATION

Thirty-eight Combined Elementary and Secondary Schools

	Total Cubature	Pupil Stations	Mean Cubature per Pupil Station
Auditorium	1,373,652	7,355	186.76
Gymnasium	1,139,306	1,215	937.70
Auditorium-gymnasium	2,332,627	2,091	1,115.56
Bleachers	291,283	2,978	97.81
Cafeteria	520,894	3,882	134.18

The weighted pupil station equivalents of the various types of pupil station are summarized in Table 14.

Number of weighted pupil stations and cost per weighted pupil station. The total number of weighted pupil stations and the cost per weighted pupil station were then calculated for each of the thirty-eight combined elementary and secondary school buildings. The total number of pupil stations in class-

Table 14

WEIGHTED PUPIL STATION EQUIVALENT OF VARIOUS TYPES
OF PUPIL STATION

Thirty-eight Combined Elementary and Secondary Schools

Pupil Station	Weighted Pupil Station Equivalent
Classroom station, 16.5 sq. ft.	1.00
Classroom station, 25.0 sq. ft.	1.52
Classroom station, 35.0 sq. ft.	2.12
Classroom station, 50.0 sq. ft.	3.03
Library	1.52
Study hall	1.00
Library-Study hall	1.52
Auditorium	.94
Gymnasium	4.74
Auditorium-Gymnasium	5.63
Bleachers	.49
Cafeteria	.68

rooms having 25 square feet per pupil station was multiplied by 1.52, the total number of pupil stations in laboratories was multiplied by 2.12, and the total number of pupil stations in shops was multiplied by 3.03. Similarly the total number of pupil stations in each library, study hall, library-study hall, auditorium, gymnasium, auditorium-gymnasium, bleacher section, and cafeteria was multiplied, respectively, by 1.52, 1.00, 1.52, .94, 4.74, 5.63, .49, or .68. The sum of these products and the number of ordinary classroom pupil stations was obtained for each building. These sums represented the number of weighted pupil stations for each building. The total cost of each building was then divided by the total number of weighted pupil stations. The resulting quotients were the costs per weighted pupil station for the buildings.

Testing the weighted pupil station unit. The new measure of building size or capacity, number of weighted pupil stations, and the new unit of cost, cost per weighted pupil station, were then subjected to the same tests of relationship which were used in the study of the first nine units. The results are shown in Table 15, Column A.

The zero order correlation coefficient of .92 for the relationship between total number of weighted pupil stations and total cost showed that number of weighted pupil stations is not as good a basis for estimating the cost of a proposed building as total cubature. This was confirmed by the average percentage of difference of 13.2 per cent between actual total construction cost and estimated total construction cost when number of weighted pupil stations was used as a basis for estimating the costs of twenty-five schools. Cost per weighted pupil station was not highly correlated with measures of efficiency of designing and planning affecting the size and shape of a building.[1] Cost per weighted pupil station had a zero order correlation of —.26 with ratio of perimeter to ground area, —.39 with ratio of perimeter to total cubature, and —.34 with ratio of ground area to total cubature. The negative signs of these correlations are discussed in a later section of this chapter. The multiple correlation coefficient was .42. Cost per weighted pupil station and per cent of habitable cubature had a zero order correlation of —.57. The highest correlation coefficient of the other nine units was —.74. Compared with the other unit costs, costs per weighted pupil station had a relatively high inverse correlation with efficiency of designing and planning affecting the per cent of habitable cubature in a building. Cost per weighted pupil station also had a relatively high inverse correlation with measures of educational serviceability. The zero order correlation between cost per weighted pupil station and per cent of educa-

[1] For a description and discussion of measures of efficiency of designing and planning used in this study, see pp. 41 to 42.

Table 15

WEIGHTED PUPIL STATIONS

	A	B
Zero order correlation between number of weighted pupil stations and total cost *	.92	.91
Average per cent of difference between actual total construction cost and estimated total construction cost **	13.2	14.5
Zero order correlation between cost per weighted pupil station and ratio of perimeter to ground area of a building *	—.26	—.26
Zero order correlation between cost per weighted pupil station and ratio of perimeter of building to total cubature *	—.39	—.38
Zero order correlation between cost per weighted pupil station and ratio of ground area of building to total cubature *	—.34	—.33
Multiple correlation between cost per weighted pupil station and three ratios measuring building shape *..	.41	.40
Zero order correlation between cost per weighted pupil station and per cent of habitable cubature *	—.57	—.56
Zero order correlation between cost per weighted pupil station and per cent of educational cubature *	—.69	—.69
Zero order correlation between cost per weighted pupil station and per cent of educational floor area *	—.76	—.77
Multiple correlation between cost per weighted pupil station and per cent of educational cubature and per cent of educational floor area *	.79	.79
Zero order correlation between number of weighted pupil stations and Score Card rating *	.91	.92

A = Pupil stations weighted in terms of area and cubature.
B = Pupil stations weighted in terms of area, cubature, and cost per cubic foot.
  * Thirty-eight combined elementary and secondary schools.
** Twenty-five combined elementary and secondary schools.

tional cubature was —.69, and between cost per weighted pupil station and per cent of educational floor area —.76. The multiple correlation for this dual relationship was .79. This compares favorably with the multiple correlation coefficient of .83 for cost per cubic foot of educational cubature, the highest of the nine original units studied. It was also found that the total number of weighted pupil stations had a correlation of .91 with

Score Card rating, indicating that number of weighted pupil stations is also a good measure of educational serviceability.

In general, cost per weighted pupil station is a desirable unit to use for comparing school building construction costs. It is superior to the un-weighted pupil station unit.

Further weighting of the pupil station unit. The pupil stations were next further weighted in terms of differences in cubic foot costs. It would have been especially fortunate if differences in cubic foot costs were known for each type of pupil station. Such information is, however, not available. The nearest approach is found in the study of school building costs by Engelhardt, Jr. [6] He found that, for the buildings studied, the general construction cost increased $.236 with each cubic foot increase in habitable space other than auditorium and gymnasium space and $.343 with each cubic foot increase in auditorium and gymnasium space. Cubature in auditoriums and gymnasiums was, therefore, found to be approximately 1.45 times as expensive as cubature in other habitable spaces.

The weighted pupil station equivalents of auditorium, gymnasium, auditorium-gymnasium, and bleacher stations were, accordingly, further weighted by multiplying each by 1.45. The number of pupil stations, further weighted in terms of cubic foot costs, was then calculated for each building. The corresponding costs per further-weighted pupil station were also determined by dividing the cost of each building by the total number of further-weighted pupil stations in the building.

Testing the further-weighted pupil station unit. The further-weighted pupil station and the cost per further-weighted pupil station were then subjected to the same tests of relationship which were used in the study of the other units. The results are shown in Table 15, Column B.

The correlation coefficients obtained were very similar to those obtained for the first weighted pupil station unit.

Reversal in sign of correlations. The nine unit costs first studied were, in general, positively correlated with the three ratios: perimeter to ground area, perimeter to total cubature, and ground area to total cubature. This is reasonable because unit costs are expected to increase as the amount of exterior wall required to enclose a given amount of cubature increases, as a building becomes more spread out, or as building height decreases and amount of roof required to cover a given amount of cubature increases. Cost per pupil, cost per weighted pupil station, and cost per further-weighted pupil station, however, followed a directly opposite trend. They were found to be negatively correlated with the three ratios.

This reversal in sign may be accounted for by a series of related circumstances. The three ratios: perimeter to ground area, perimeter to total cubature, and ground area to total cubature, were negatively correlated with size of building, as measured by total cubature. In other words, the larger buildings tended to have lower ratios of perimeter to ground area, perimeter to total cubature, and ground area to total cubature. That is, the larger buildings required less outside wall per unit of cubature enclosed; they were less spread out; and they were higher. But these larger buildings also tended to have more cubature per pupil, per weighted pupil station, and per further-weighted pupil station than the smaller buildings. This was due to the fact that the larger buildings included a greater proportion of special rooms and facilities, such as boys' corrective exercise room, girls' corrective exercise room, bicycle room, teachers' dining room, assistant principal's office, music teacher's office, art teacher's office, radio room, ticket room, check room, physical instructor's office and private shower, model apartment, waiting rooms for offices, vault, men teachers' room, women teachers' room, oral hygiene clinic, and team rooms. Some of these special facilities are reflected in pupil station analyses and some are not. The inclusion of these special rooms in the larger buildings increased their cost per pupil, cost per weighted pupil station, and cost per further-weighted pupil station more than their other unit costs.[2] For

2 The correlation coefficient expressing the relationship between size of building, as measured by total cubature, and cost per pupil was .28. Cost per weighted pupil station and cost per further-weighted pupil station, when correlated with total cubature, each had a correlation coefficient of .53. No other unit cost studied was significantly correlated with size of building.

this reason higher costs per pupil, per weighted pupil station, and per further-weighted pupil station were associated with lower values of the three ratios: perimeter to ground area, perimeter to total cubature, and ground area to total cubature.

Further refinement of the weighted pupil station unit. Further research is needed to establish area and cubature standards for various types of pupil station. Detailed studies of space utilization and space needs for every type of pupil station should be made in order to provide the necessary data for more accurate weighting.

As buildings become larger, many special rooms are provided which are not considered in estimating the number of weighted pupil stations. Such rooms include: medical suite, dental suite, men teachers' room, assistant principal's office, guidance office, music teacher's office, art teacher's office, physical directors' offices with shower and toilet rooms, and visiting team rooms. These facilities add to the value as well as the cost of the actual pupil stations. In further refinement of the weighted pupil station unit, it may be possible to assign weighted pupil station equivalents to some or all rooms not at present counted in pupil station analyses or to vary the weighting of the pupil stations in accordance with the number and type of these additional facilities.

It must also be recognized that pupil stations differ one from another in the number and type of electrical and plumbing outlets and fixtures required. The plumbing and electrical installations for various types of pupil station, however, have not yet been standardized. For example, the amount of cubature required for a laboratory pupil station is definitely established for present construction in New York State, but the number of electrical and plumbing outlets varies from school to school. Further research is needed in this area.

Summary. Cost per weighted pupil station proved to be a desirable unit to use for comparing school building construction costs. It was superior to the un-weighted pupil station unit.

Cost per weighted pupil station was inversely related to efficiency of designing and planning affecting the per cent of habitable cubature in a building.

Cost per weighted pupil station was also inversely related to measures of educational serviceability. The higher the per cent of educational cubature and per cent of educational floor area, the lower the cost per weighted pupil station.

The total number of weighted pupil stations in a building was highly correlated with Score Card rating. Total number of weighted pupil stations, therefore, proved to be a good measure of the educational serviceability of a building.

Refinement of the weighted pupil station unit is dependent upon further research to establish area and cubature standards for all types of pupil station. Such research will make possible a more accurate weighting of the pupil stations. It may be possible also to find a way to assign weighted pupil station equivalents to some or all rooms not at present counted in pupil station analyses or to vary the weighting of the pupil stations in accordance with the number and type of these additional facilities.

Chapter X

Summary, Conclusions, and Recommendations

Introduction. In a monograph, *Research Problems in School Finance,* the National Survey of School Finance stressed the need for research directed toward the improvement of existing units of expenditure measurement in school finance and the development of unit expenditure measures related to specific categories of service. In spite of the large expenditures of money for school building construction, the number of research studies of school building costs has been surprisingly small. In view of the limited amount of research which had been carried on and the areas in which that research had been conducted, a study of unit cost measures for school building construction seemed to be needed. Such a study appeared to be in line with recommendations of the National Survey of School Finance because the study would aim to improve existing units of expenditure measurement and to develop possible new expenditure measures for school building construction costs. Knowledge derived from such a study seemed to be basic to an understanding of the values and limitations of the units in terms of which other cost studies might be made. Preliminary investigation disclosed that architects and educators had long been dissatisfied with some of the units used for expressing and comparing school building costs. These men felt that some of the units commonly used failed to provide a fair basis for comparing school building costs.

Comparative cost data. Lack of well-defined, clearly understood, and generally accepted units of expenditure measurement has made comparative study of school building costs difficult. Adequate and valid cost data must be secured and used "not only for immediate needs but also over a long-time period for comparative studies." [8 : 309] School building costs must be studied "to enable boards of education to provide with some degree of accuracy sufficient funds for the erection and equipment of new buildings" and "to determine, by comparison with the costs of similar structures, before the board has obligated itself by contracts, the economy to be exercised in the planning and construction of the proposed work." [11 : 70]

Literature of unit costs of school buildings. A review of the literature of unit costs revealed that at least nine units of measure have been used or proposed for measuring the size or capacity of school buildings. The measures of size or capacity resulting from the application of these units of measure are:

1. Total cubature
2. Habitable cubature
3. Educational cubature
4. Total floor area
5. Habitable floor area
6. Educational floor area
7. Number of classrooms
8. Pupil capacity
9. Number of pupil stations

Unit costs indicate the cost of school building construction per unit of size or capacity. The units of cost corresponding to the measures listed above are:

1. Cost per cubic foot
2. Cost per cubic foot of habitable cubature
3. Cost per cubic foot of educational cubature
4. Cost per square foot of floor area
5. Cost per square foot of habitable floor area
6. Cost per square foot of educational floor area
7. Cost per classroom
8. Cost per pupil
9. Cost per pupil station

A summary was made of statements of the advantages and disadvantages of the various units. This summary was based on criticisms appearing in books, magazine articles, and published speeches. These statements were not always in agreement.

The purpose of the study. The purpose of this study has been to evaluate in an impartial, objective manner the nine measures of building size or capacity and the nine units of cost mentioned above. There was no published evidence of any attempt to do this previously. The study has attempted to answer the following questions:

1. What are the advantages and disadvantages of the various units applied to school building costs?

2. Which measure of building size or capacity is best suited for use in estimating the cost of a proposed building?

3. Which unit of cost is best suited for comparing school building costs?

4. Can a new unit be developed which will be more satisfactory than those now used?

Buildings studied. At the time this study was planned, Engelhardt, Jr. was contemplating a study of school buildings in New York State in an effort to discover the elements of design and construction which were related to variations in the cost of these buildings. It was anticipated that the findings of Engelhardt, Jr. could be utilized to correct the total costs of the buildings so that the effects of certain construction factors would be eliminated. This would facilitate the study of relationships between the unit costs and other factors. It was decided, therefore, that the same group of buildings would be used for each study.

The writer worked with Engelhardt, Jr. in gathering the basic data, with the understanding that some of these data would also be used for the writer's study which was to follow. The enormous amount of detail work involved in taking data from the plans and specifications for each building was a further justification for this procedure.

Eight elementary schools, six secondary schools, and thirty-eight combined elementary and secondary schools comprised the group of fifty-two school buildings studied. These were the school buildings constructed in New York State between

1930 and 1937 for which complete plans, specifications, and cost data were obtainable from the School Buildings and Grounds Division of the New York State Education Department. One-room and two-room buildings of wood-frame construction and additions to existing buildings were excluded.

Plan analysis. Engelhardt, Jr. and the writer, working together as described above, obtained the following basic data for each building:

1. Total cubature
2. Total floor area
3. Linear feet of perimeter of the building
4. Square feet of ground area covered by the building
5. Cubature of all rooms and spaces
6. Floor area of all rooms and spaces
7. Number of floors above basement
8. Square feet of radiation
9. Number and type of plumbing outlets and fixtures
10. Number and type of electrical outlets and fixtures
11. Type of roof
12. Basic materials of construction
13. Interior finish materials

In addition to these data, the writer determined for each building:

1. Number of classrooms
2. Pupil capacity of building
3. Number of pupil stations of various types

From these basic data the writer determined for each building:

1. Total habitable cubature
2. Total educational cubature
3. Total educational floor area
4. Per cent of habitable cubature
5. Per cent of educational cubature
6. Per cent of educational floor area
7. Ratio of perimeter to ground area
8. Ratio of perimeter to total cubature

9. Ratio of ground area to total cubature
10. Mean cubature per auditorium pupil station
11. Mean cubature per gymnasium pupil station
12. Mean cubature per auditorium-gymnasium pupil station
13. Mean cubature per bleacher pupil station
14. Mean cubature per cafeteria pupil station
15. Number of weighted pupil stations (weighted in terms of area and cubature)
16. Number of further-weighted pupil stations (weighted in terms of area, cubature, and cost per cubic foot)

Building costs. The basic cost data were obtained by Engelhardt, Jr. and the writer from the files of the School Buildings and Grounds Division of the New York State Education Department. The total cost of construction included:

1. Cost of the general construction contract
2. Cost of the heating and ventilating contract
3. Cost of the plumbing contract
4. Cost of the electrical contract
5. Other contract and non-contract costs which contributed to the expense of general construction, heating and ventilating, plumbing, or electrical work

General procedure. In order to determine which measure of building size or capacity is best suited for use in estimating the cost of a proposed building, the school buildings used in this study were measured in terms of each, and these measures were then correlated with the total costs of the buildings. As a further check on the correlations, the costs of twenty-five buildings were estimated on the basis of each measure of building size or capacity.

Unit costs of school buildings are determined, in the first instance, by quality of construction. But costs are also influenced by skillful planning. The superior architect creates a more efficient design from both a structural and an educational point of view.

The various units are not equally effective in revealing these differences in efficiency of designing and planning and in educational serviceability. Yet, this is exactly the effectiveness which is needed in a unit of cost used for comparative purposes. The best unit to use in comparing school building construction costs is the one which is most closely related to measures of efficiency of designing and planning and to measures of educational serviceability.

In this study the units of cost were studied in relation to efficiency of designing and planning of the buildings. The units of cost were correlated with four measures of efficiency of designing and planning.[1] The units of cost were also studied in relation to the educational serviceability of the buildings by correlating the units of cost with two measures of educational serviceability. The measures of building size or capacity were also correlated with a measure of educational serviceability.

Correcting the costs. In order to study the measures of building size or capacity and the units of cost as described above, it was desirable to eliminate as many as possible of the variations in costs due to other factors.

To eliminate the effect of variations in wages and materials prices, the costs of general construction, heating and ventilating, plumbing, and electrical work were corrected by means of indices developed for this group of buildings by Engelhardt, Jr. [6] Each of the four basic construction costs was corrected separately by means of the appropriate index. The four corrected costs for each building were then added to form total costs of construction corrected for variations in wages and materials prices.

These total costs were further corrected for variations due to type of construction, roof construction, and grade of interior finish. Finally, the total costs were corrected for variations due to general plan type. These corrections were based on the findings of Engelhardt, Jr. and were made in the manner which he describes. [6 : 43, 46]

These successive corrections of total costs made possible the study of the measures of building size or capacity and units of

---

[1] For a description and discussion of measures of efficiency of designing and planning used in this study, see pp. 41 to 42.

cost at three separate stages as the effects of variations due to construction factors were eliminated.

Unit costs. On the basis of total costs corrected for variations in wages and materials prices, type of construction, roof construction, and grade of interior finish, the writer calculated the following unit costs for each building:

1. Cost per cubic foot
2. Cost per cubic foot of habitable cubature
3. Cost per cubic foot of educational cubature
4. Cost per square foot of floor area
5. Cost per square foot of habitable floor area
6. Cost per square foot of educational floor area
7. Cost per classroom
8. Cost per pupil
9. Cost per pupil station
10. Cost per weighted pupil station
11. Cost per further-weighted pupil station

Unit costs were similarly calculated for each building on the basis of costs corrected for variations in wages and materials prices, type of construction, roof construction, grade of interior finish, and general plan type.

Findings. Total cubature proved to be the best measure of building size or capacity to use as a basis for estimating the cost of a proposed school building. Total cubature had the highest correlation with total cost of construction. The average percentage of difference between actual and estimated total cost of construction was lowest when total cubature was used as a basis for estimating the costs of twenty-five school buildings.

Total floor area was found to be the second best measure of building size or capacity to use as a basis for estimating the cost of a proposed school building.

The opinion that cost per cubic foot gives no indication of efficiency of planning was partly supported and partly contradicted. Contrary to the expressed opinion, compared with the other unit costs studied, cost per cubic foot was found to have a relatively high inverse correlation with efficiency of designing and planning insofar as designing and planning affect the size and shape of a building. Cost per cubic foot decreased as amount of wall required to enclose a given amount of cubature decreased, as the buildings became larger or less spread out, and as the buildings became higher. In other words, cost per cubic foot decreased as efficiency of designing and planning affecting the size and shape of a building increased. On the other hand, in support of the opinion that cost per cubic foot gives no indication of efficiency of planning, no significant relationship was found between cost per cubic foot and per cent of habitable cubature. The opinion was, therefore, partly supported and partly contradicted.

The claim that comparisons of costs of school buildings, when made on the basis of cost per cubic foot of educational cubature, reveal wasteful planning was found to be justified. The higher the per cent of habitable cubature, the less wall required to enclose a given amount of cubature, and the larger or less spread out the building, the lower the cost per cubic foot of educational cubature.

No support was found for the contention that cost per pupil station is a measure of efficiency of planning.

Cost per cubic foot of habitable cubature was found most highly related in a negative sense to efficiency of designing and planning. As efficiency of designing and planning increased, cost per cubic foot of habitable cubature decreased.

The opinion that cost per cubic foot gives no indication of the educational serviceability of a school building was confirmed by this study.

Cost per cubic foot of educational cubature, cost per square foot of educational floor area, and cost per pupil station were found to be good units of cost from the standpoint of reflecting the educational serviceability of school buildings.

Number of pupil stations was found to be most highly related to Score Card rating of the buildings.

Cost per weighted pupil station proved to be a desirable unit to use for comparing school building construction costs. It was superior to the un-weighted pupil station unit.

Cost per weighted pupil station was inversely related to efficiency of designing and planning affecting the per cent of habitable cubature in a building.

Cost per weighted pupil station was also inversely related to measures of educational serviceability. The higher the per cent of educational cubature and per cent of educational floor area, the lower the cost per weighted pupil station.

Compared with the other measures of building size or capacity studied, the total number of weighted pupil stations in a building was relatively highly correlated with Score Card rating. Total number of weighted pupil stations proved to be a good measure of educational serviceability.

Conclusions. Total cubature is the best measure of building size or capacity to use for estimating the cost of a proposed school building. Such estimates should be based on known costs of similar buildings. Cost per cubic foot is an unsatisfactory unit of cost to use for comparing school building costs.

Cost per cubic foot of habitable cubature is the best unit to use for comparing costs in terms of efficiency of designing and planning.

Cost per cubic foot of educational cubature, cost per square foot of educational floor area, and cost per weighted pupil station are the best units to use for comparing school building costs in terms of educational serviceability.

The results of this study support the point of view expressed by Lambert:

. . . unit-cost studies to be significant should be multiple studies in which the results obtained by one specific unit will illuminate the results obtained by applying other units. A cost study should be made for a specific purpose and the results should be interpreted in the light of that purpose. Otherwise, so-called unit-cost studies will only promote confusion. There is not yet any single best denominator to use for making unit-cost analyses of school expenditures. [24 : 65]

Applicability of the study. Some of the statements made in the past concerning units applied to school building costs were found untenable because they were not in agreement with the facts adduced by this study. It cannot be assumed, however, that statements regarding the units which were found to be true, when tested by the data of this study, are necessarily universally true.

The number of school buildings studied was, of necessity, limited. This was due in part to the difficulty of gaining access to a large number of complete plans and specifications, in part to the enormous amount of detail work involved in getting the data from the plans and specifications, but chiefly to the need for restricting the study to the school buildings of one state in order that some of the variables associated with costs of school buildings could be held constant.

The group of New York State buildings studied was not a random sample of all school buildings in other states. Many of the buildings in other states are built under varying physical conditions and are designed to fulfill different educational needs and programs. Although this fact suggests a need for caution in drawing inferences from this study regarding use of certain units of cost for other groups of school buildings, the applicability of the study is not as restricted as might, at first, be supposed.

The New York State buildings used in this study are reasonably representative of current school building construction. They conform to accepted standards of safety and sanitation. They are attractive in appearance and sound in construction. It is reasonable to assume that measures of building size or capacity and units of cost found suitable for these buildings will prove equally helpful in studying the costs of other groups of school buildings built in recent years.

Practical considerations. Several practical considerations govern the applicability of the results of the study. In general, comparisons of school building costs should be made in statewide studies. If the units are applied to school buildings in each state separately, the unit costs are not affected by differences in legal requirements governing building construction or the educational program. Even climate is fairly uniform in its demands on building construction within each state.

Also, before unit cost comparisons are made, school building costs should be corrected by means of appropriate indices to eliminate the effect of fluctuations in labor and materials prices. Unusual conditions affecting the costs of foundations should also be considered, and proper adjustments in cost should be made. Furthermore, inasmuch as the costs of sites vary considerably from one community to another and even in different parts of the same community, site costs should not be included when school building costs are compared.

Comparisons should ordinarily be made with buildings on the same educational level. Unit costs of elementary school buildings should be compared with those of other elementary schools; unit costs of secondary school buildings should be compared with those of other secondary schools; and unit costs of combined elementary and secondary school buildings should be compared with those of other combined elementary and secondary schools.

Norms of expenditure. No attempt was made to establish norms of expenditure. The relative economy or extravagance of expenditures cannot be determined solely on the basis of cost. The price paid for expensive school buildings may be fully justified. Higher initial cost may result in lower operating and maintenance costs. Higher cost may provide accommodations resulting in superior educational accomplishments and richer community life. Higher cost may represent the differential between adequate and inadequate adaptation of construction to curricular needs and community use. Higher cost may result in a finer aesthetic interpretation of the function of education. Or the reverse may be true.

Opportunities for further research. There are many opportunities for further research in the field of unit costs of school buildings. Statewide comparative studies of school building costs, studies of operation and maintenance costs in relation to initial construction costs, and studies of costs of essential educational service facilities are needed. In fact, the many problems associated with costs of school building construction make the establishment of a continuing program of research in this area of the utmost importance.

More closely related to the present study is the need for research directed toward the refinement of area and cubature standards for various types of pupil station. Detailed studies of space utilization and space needs should be made.

It may also be possible to develop weighted pupil station equivalents for space in some or all rooms not at present counted in pupil station analyses, or it may be possible to vary the weighting of the present pupil stations in accordance with the number and type of these additional facilities.

The weighted pupil station unit is worthy of further study and refinement as a basis for estimating the cost of a proposed school building. Its special advantage lies in the fact that it makes possible the estimating of costs on the basis of a statement of need before any plans are drawn.

Concluding statement. This study summarizes the theory of unit costs applied to school building construction. This theory has been developing over a period of about twenty-five years. The study contradicts some of the statements found in the literature of unit costs of school buildings and substantiates others; it presents evidence regarding the relative merits of measures of building size or capacity for estimating construction costs of proposed buildings and units of cost for comparing construction costs of school buildings.

This study shows the folly of continuing to make comparisons of school building costs solely on the basis of cost per cubic foot. School building costs should be compared in terms of not one unit of cost, but several.

This study also shows the advantages of using other units of cost as bases for comparative cost studies. These other units are more desirable than the cost per cubic foot unit for this purpose because they reveal differences in cost in relation to efficiency of designing and planning and in relation to the educational serviceability of school buildings. Cost data for many schools, expressed in such units, should be made available so that architects and educators may be able to study the cost of a proposed building against a background of comparable experience.

Those responsible for the construction of school buildings should seek to determine for each new building project (1) whether the cost will be relatively high or low compared with the costs of similar buildings, (2) if the cost is exceptionally high or low, what are the underlying causes of this unusual cost, and (3) whether the cost can be justified on the basis of the quality of construction of the building and its potential usefulness.

The sum total of many appraisals of costs of school buildings made in this way in various states and local communities will constitute a widespread and significant study of school building costs. Such independent analyses may or may not bring about a reduction in school building costs, but they will surely result in a greater return for each dollar spent in school building construction. Such appraisals of costs will result in the construction of better buildings for the same or less money. This is the essence of true economy.

Bibliography

1. The Research Staff of the National Survey of School Finance and Special Consultants. *Research Problems in School Finance.* The American Council on Education, Washington, D. C., 1933.
2. U. S. Office of Education. *Biennial Survey of Education.* Bulletin, 1937, No. 2, Vol. II, Chap. II, p. 33, Government Printing Office, Washington, D. C., 1939.
3. The University of the State of New York, The State Education Department. *Thirty-fourth Annual Report of the Education Department.* Vol. 2, Statistics. Albany, N. Y., 1939.
4. Bormann, Henry H. and Engelhardt, Jr., N. L. "Cost of School Buildings." *Review of Educational Research.* Vol. VIII, pp. 408-412, 480-481, October, 1938.
5. Herber, Howard T. *The Influence of the Public Works Administration on School Building Construction in New York State.* Contributions to Education, No. 762. Bureau of Publications, Teachers College, Columbia University, New York, 1938.
6. Engelhardt, Jr., N. L. *School Building Costs.* Bureau of Publications, Teachers College, Columbia University, New York, 1939.
7. Ittner, William B. "The Cost of School Buildings." *American School Board Journal,* Vol. 51, pp. 17, 69, August, 1915.
8. Moehlman, Arthur B. "The Theory of School-Plant Costs." In *The Planning and Construction of School Buildings. Thirty-third Yearbook of the National Society for the Study of Education,* Part I (Guy M. Whipple, edr.). Public School Publishing Company, Bloomington, Ill., 1934.
9. Collins, D. C. Newman. "The Cost of School Buildings." *American School Board Journal,* Vol. 49, pp. 19, 61-62, September, 1914.
10. Baldwin, Edward C. "The Cost of Schoolhouse Construction, with a Proposed Unit Based on Cubical Contents." ' *Heating and Ventilating Magazine,* Vol. 12, pp. 22-27, June, 1915.
11. Donovan, John J. *School Architecture: Principles and Practices.* The Macmillan Company, New York, 1921.
12. Shigley, Arthur R. "Acquainting the Layman with School Building Costs." *Nation's Schools,* Vol. 5, pp. 39-43, March, 1930.
13. Steen, M. M. "Comparative Cubage." In *Proceedings of the Twenty-fourth Annual Meeting of the National Association of Public School Business Officials,* pp. 112-118. Published by the Association, 1935.

14. Wooldridge, C. L. "Can School Building Costs Be Made Comparative?" In *Proceedings of the Twenty-fourth Annual Meeting of the National Association of Public School Business Officials*, pp. 108-111. Published by the Association, 1935.

15. Greeley, W. R. "Schoolhouses in Massachusetts." *Architectural Forum*, Vol. 33, pp. 155-160, November, 1920.

16. Kilham, Walter H. "The Modern Schoolhouse. Cubage and Cost." *Brickbuilder*, Vol. 24, pp. 107-110, May, 1915.

17. Wiley, G. E. "Comparing School-Building Costs." *American School Board Journal*, Vol. 90, pp. 17-19, January, 1935.

18. Halsey, R. H. F. "What Unit Should Be Used for Cost Comparison of Schoolhouses?" In *Proceedings of the Twelfth Annual Meeting of the National Council on Schoolhouse Construction*, pp. 18-23. Published by the Council, Nashville, Tenn., 1934.

19. *American School Board Journal*. "Unit Costs of School Buildings." Vol. 74, pp. 60, 162, May, 1927.

20. Morse, Herbert N. and Anderson, Charles D. "Method of Computing and Comparing School-Building Costs." *American School and University*, Vol. 2, pp. 22-25. American School Publishing Corporation, New York, 1929.

21. Betelle, J. O. "School Building Construction Costs." *Architectural Forum*, Vol. 37, pp. 77-79, August, 1922.

22. Engelhardt, N. L. and Engelhardt, Fred. *Planning School Building Programs*. Bureau of Publications, Teachers College, Columbia University, New York, 1930.

23. Strayer, G. D. and Engelhardt, N. L. *Standards for High School Buildings*. Bureau of Publications, Teachers College, Columbia University, New York, 1924.

24. Lambert, A. C. "The Useful Units for Making Analyses of School Costs." *American School Board Journal*, Vol. 80, pp. 65, 134, May, 1930.

VITA

HENRY HUBENER BORMANN was born in Brooklyn, New York, October 20, 1905. He received his pre-college education in schools of the City of New York and won a New York State Regents Scholarship upon graduation from Newtown High School in June, 1922. In June, 1926, he received the degree of bachelor of science, *cum laude*, with honors in mathematics, from University College of Arts and Pure Science, New York University. Two years later he received the degree of master of arts from the School of Education, New York University.

From September, 1926, to June, 1929, he taught mathematics and history in Malverne High School, Malverne, New York. Since 1929, he has been principal of two elementary schools in East Rockaway, New York.

He has been elected to membership in the honorary fraternities of Phi Beta Kappa, Phi Delta Kappa, and Kappa Delta Pi. He is a past-president of the Nassau County Schoolmen's Association and president of the New York State Association of Elementary School Principals.

He is the author of *Bridges*, published in 1934 by The Macmillan Company; co-author of Bulletin V, *The Informal Daily Program*, published in 1937 by the New York State Association of Elementary School Principals; and co-author of *An Elementary School Inventory*, published in 1940 by the New York State Education Department.